The Psych 101 Series

James C. Kaufman, PhD, Series Editor
Department of Educational Psychology
University of Connecticut

Karin Sternberg, PhD, did her undergraduate and graduate work at the University of Heidelberg, Germany. Work leading to her PhD, awarded summa cum laude, was done under Professor Manfred Amelang at Heidelberg. Dr. Sternberg did her postdoctoral work in social psychology at the University of Connecticut. She also has an MBA degree. Dr. Sternberg (née Weis) is coeditor of *The New Psychology of Love* (2006) and coauthor of *The Psychology of Hate* (2008). She is also senior author of "The Nature of Love," which appeared in *21st Century Psychology: A Reference Handbook* (2008), and of "Love," which will appear in *The Encyclopedia of the Mind* (in press). In addition, Karin Sternberg is coauthor of *The Psychologist's Companion* (Fifth ed., 2010) and *Cognitive Psychology* (Sixth ed., 2012).

Dr. Sternberg is principal of Sternberg Consulting and an adjunct assistant professor of psychology at the University of Wyoming.

Psychology of Love 101

Karin Sternberg, PhD

SPRINGER PUBLISHING COMPANY
NEW YORK

Copyright © 2014 Springer Publishing Company, LLC

All rights reserved.

No part of this publication may be reproduced, stored in a retrieval system, or transmitted in any form or by any means, electronic, mechanical, photocopying, recording, or otherwise, without the prior permission of Springer Publishing Company, LLC, or authorization through payment of the appropriate fees to the Copyright Clearance Center, Inc., 222 Rosewood Drive, Danvers, MA 01923, 978-750-8400, fax 978-646-8600, info@copyright.com or on the Web at www.copyright.com.

Springer Publishing Company, LLC
11 West 42nd Street
New York, NY 10036
www.springerpub.com

Acquisitions Editor: Nancy S. Hale
Composition: Amnet

ISBN: 978-0-8261-0935-4
e-book ISBN: 978-0-8261-0933-0

13 14 15 16 / 5 4 3 2 1

The author and the publisher of this Work have made every effort to use sources believed to be reliable to provide information that is accurate and compatible with the standards generally accepted at the time of publication. The author and publisher shall not be liable for any special, consequential, or exemplary damages resulting, in whole or in part, from the readers' use of, or reliance on, the information contained in this book. The publisher has no responsibility for the persistence or accuracy of URLs for external or third-party Internet websites referred to in this publication and does not guarantee that any content on such websites is, or will remain, accurate or appropriate.

Library of Congress Cataloging-in-Publication Data

Sternberg, Karin, 1976–
  Psychology of love 101 / Karin Sternberg, PhD.
     pages cm.—(Psych 101)
  Includes bibliographical references and index.
  ISBN 978-0-8261-0935-4 (print edition : alk. paper)—
  ISBN 978-0-8261-0933-0 (e-book) 1. Love.   2. Interpersonal attraction.
3. Interpersonal relations.   I. Title.
  BF575.L8S778 2014
  152.4′1—dc23   2013028322

Special discounts on bulk quantities of our books are available to corporations, professional associations, pharmaceutical companies, health care organizations, and other qualifying groups. If you are interested in a custom book, including chapters from more than one of our titles, we can provide that service as well.

For details, please contact:
Special Sales Department, Springer Publishing Company, LLC
11 West 42nd Street, 15th Floor, New York, NY 10036-8002
Phone: 877-687-7476 or 212-431-4370; Fax: 212-941-7842
E-mail: sales@springerpub.com

Printed in the United States of America by Gasch Printing.

To Bob
and Samuel, Brittany, and Melody:
the loves of my life

Contents

Preface ix

Chapter 1 Introduction: The Nature of Love 1

Chapter 2 Love From a Biological Perspective 15

Chapter 3 Are There Different Kinds of Love? Taxonomic Approaches 35

Chapter 4 Cultural Theories of Love 59

Chapter 5 A Primer on Methods: Constructing a Love Scale 77

Chapter 6 Interpersonal Attraction 91

Chapter 7 Stages of Relationships: How Relationships Are Formed, Maintained, and Ended 111

Chapter 8 Online Dating 131

CONTENTS

Chapter 9   Love and Personality   151

Chapter 10   Relationship Challenges:
Questions and Answers   163

References   173
Index   197

Preface

enator William Proxmire, many years ago, awarded two psychological researchers, Elaine Hatfield and Ellen Berscheid, a "Golden Fleece Award" for studying love psychologically. He argued that some things cannot be understood scientifically, and love is one of them. The senator was poking fun at them, but his fun came at a great cost to the researchers, who had to stave off criticism from many others who were simply following the lead of the senator. Hatfield and Berscheid proved the senator, who had no scientific credentials, wrong. They went on to make tremendous contributions to the scientific study of love, winning the highest honors in the field of psychology from both the American Psychological Association and the Association for Psychological Science.

This book probably would not have been possible without the work of Hatfield and Berscheid, who proved to many subsequent researchers that the scientific study of love is indeed possible. This book presents in an informal and readable style much of what scientists have learned about love during the past half century or so. The book covers both theories and data, and provides a comprehensive grounding in the psychology of love. But because the book is intended for interested laypeople and students, it is written in a way that anyone can understand, even someone who has never taken a psychology course.

PREFACE

Some years ago I coedited a book titled *The New Psychology of Love*. The book contained truly fascinating chapters describing a wide variety of approaches to love. But the book was written primarily for scholars, and I could not help feeling that it simply would not be accessible to many laypeople, including students, who wanted to know about love but needed an introduction that was not quite so technical. When James Kaufman, the series editor of the Psych 101 series, asked me to write this book, I knew the opportunity had come for me to present the new psychology of love, but in a more accessible way.

The basic thesis of this book is that scientific research can help us all in our loving relationships. Consequently, the book talks not only about theory and data, but also about how to apply them to our close relationships. One chapter provides questions and answers about loving relationships, based on scientific research. Another chapter discusses online dating and the issue of just what we can expect when we meet people online. Yet another chapter provides questions and answers that will put the research discussed in the book into practice. You will find, therefore, that *Psychology of Love 101* is not only a brief text, but also a book that will help you clarify how scientific research can matter in your life. The complete "Triangular Love Scale" is presented in Chapter 5 and will enable you to analyze in some detail the levels of intimacy, passion, and commitment in your relationships. The scale, based on psychological theory and validated using large numbers of participants, will show you how psychologists not only construct theories, but also translate these theories into measures that can assess scientifically the phenomena they study.

The book considers most of the standard topics in the psychology of love, covering research primarily about heterosexual but also about gay couples. It describes different kinds of love, including the kinds that are more likely to lead to relationship success and also the kinds associated with relationship failure. It specifically discusses factors that lead to greater or lesser success, as well as personality variables and their associations with different kinds of love. While the book focuses mainly on romantic love, it also covers other aspects of love, such as parental love and friendship.

One of the most difficult challenges in life is figuring out whether a relationship is really working. It truly helps, in doing so, to have a thorough grounding in psychological theories of love. Such theories can enable you to analyze your love relationship from a variety of psychological standpoints and to evaluate whether the relationship is providing you with the amount and type of love you are seeking.

I hope you enjoy reading this book as much as I enjoyed writing it. I am lucky in my life to have found love in many places. I come from a loving family and have a wonderful husband, Bob, and beautiful triplets—Samuel, Brittany, and Melody. I want to thank my extended family—my parents, Helge and Brigitte; my sister, Petra; and my husband and triplets—for giving me the support through my life that made this book possible. I hope this book helps you find in your life the happiness through love I have found in mine.

Creativity 101
James C. Kaufman, PhD

Genius 101
Dean Keith Simonton, PhD

IQ Testing 101
Alan S. Kaufman, PhD

Leadership 101
Michael D. Mumford, PhD

Anxiety 101
Moshe Zeidner, PhD
Gerald Matthews, PhD

Psycholinguistics 101
H. Wind Cowles, PhD

Humor 101
Mitch Earleywine, PhD

Obesity 101
Lauren Rossen, PhD
Eric Rossen, PhD

Emotional Intelligence 101
Gerald Matthews, PhD
Moshe Zeidner, PhD
Richard D. Roberts, PhD

Personality 101
Gorkan Ahmetoglu, PhD
Tomas Chamorro-Premuzic, PhD

Giftedness 101
Linda Kreger Silverman, PhD

Evolutionary Psychology 101
Glenn Geher, PhD

Psychology of Love 101
Karin Sternberg, PhD

Intelligence 101
Jonathan Plucker, PhD
Amber Esping, PhD

Depression 101
C. Emily Durbin, PhD

Psychology of Love
101

Introduction: The Nature of Love

"I love you," John says to Jane. "I love you," Jane says to John. John and Jane get married and plan to live happily ever after.

John and Jane split up.

"I thought you loved me," Jane says to John.

"I did," John replies to Jane.

"But love is forever," Jane retorts to John.

"Not for me it isn't," John replies, hanging up the phone.

What is love, anyway? And is it the same thing for everyone, or is it different things for different people, as with John and Jane?

Like most people, including John and Jane, I spent more time than I wished in love relationships that proved to be less successful than I hoped they would be. Then, finally, I was fortunate enough to find the relationship of my dreams. Throughout this whole process I, like so many others, have wondered: What exactly is love? Why is it so hard to find? And what is it that makes two people compatible in a loving relationship, or else destines the relationship to failure? Although this book will not definitively answer each of these questions, it will go a long way toward this end by addressing them.

WHY IS LOVE IMPORTANT?

For many people, love is the most important thing in their lives. Most of us have the love of our family of origin, but we want something more—to find the love of our life, the person with whom we will happily spend the rest of our days. Even people who are very oriented toward other endeavors—career, travel, athletics, various kinds of adventures—seek love to enrich and in many ways transform their lives. Love is vital not only to our self-fulfillment, but also to the propagation of future generations. At least for humans, without love the future of the species would be grim indeed. Even if couples produced children under conditions lacking love, growing up without love would doom many of these children to lives of great unhappiness and would jeopardize the future for us all.

Although love is of the utmost importance to many if not most of us, people interested in love have not always been encouraged to study it. For example, in 1974, then-Senator William Proxmire of Wisconsin bestowed upon two professors, Ellen Berscheid at the University of Minnesota and Elaine Hatfield at the University of Wisconsin, what he called a Golden Fleece Award, claiming that their National Science Foundation–supported research on why people fall in love was fleecing the country's taxpayers. Proxmire failed to realize that the only way to understand phenomena in our lives is to study them.

He started a tradition of politicians castigating researchers for research that the politicians did not appreciate and, often, did not understand.

APPROACHES TO STUDYING LOVE

There is no one "right" approach to studying love. Students of love have, at different times in different places, taken a variety of approaches to understanding what love is. Let's consider some of the major approaches.

Philosophical Approaches

Perhaps the earliest approach to understanding the nature of love was through philosophy. One of the first known philosophers, Plato, devoted much of his dialogue *Symposium* to a consideration of different views on love. Phaedrus, for example, notes how lovers may sacrifice their lives for their love. The type of love to which he refers has come to be called *agape*, a sacrificing type of love where one puts the well-being of one's lover ahead of one's own well-being. Pausanias distinguishes between earthly and heavenly love. Heavenly love emphasizes the intellect and enduring commitment, whereas earthly love is more lustful. What he called heavenly love came to be called *storge* by some theorists, and what he called earthly love came to be called *eros*. These constructs endure even today.

The great advantage of the philosophical approach is that it brings some of the best minds in human history, such as Plato and Aristotle, to bear upon understanding the nature of love. These are minds that offer insights that few others in human history would be capable of. A limitation of the approach, for some people, is that it seems speculative. For other people, reading philosophy is just too dry or dull for them to become engaged. This, of course, may say more about the people than it does about the material. A juicier approach is perhaps through literature.

Literary Approaches

Probably no topic has garnered more attention in literature than love. English authors such as Geoffrey Chaucer, William Shakespeare, Emily and Charlotte Brontë, and Jane Austen have written about love. So have French authors such as Honoré de Balzac, Victor Hugo, and Albert Camus; Russian authors such as Fyodor Dostoyevsky and Leo Tolstoy; Latin American authors such as Gabriel García Márquez and Julio Cortázar; and North American authors such as F. Scott Fitzgerald, Ernest Hemingway, and Toni Morrison. Some people feel that they learn more about love from reading the works of these great authors than they learn from nonfiction books on love. García Márquez's *Love in the Time of Cholera* is one of the great explorations of love in any language.

Literature has had a tremendous effect on our understanding of love. Shakespeare has been more influential, at least in Western thinking about love, than perhaps anyone else. For example, *Romeo and Juliet* is a timeless classic that illustrates the hardships of love across families that, for one reason or another, detest each other. *Othello* shows what happens when jealousy fired by love takes a disastrous turn. *King Lear* shows what happens when a family experiences both love and the attempt to feign it. The greatest advantage of the literary approach is its richness and its ability to show love in all of its nearly infinite varieties. Perhaps the greatest disadvantage of this approach is that it is hard to get a handle on the nature of love through literature. What exactly is love, or what are the types of love? There is no easy guide to deconstructing literature to ascertain the precise message of each individual author. Moreover, some will ask to what extent someone sitting in an armchair (or wherever) truly can discern the nature of a construct as important as love. As a result, some students of love have turned to other approaches. One is what we might call a "pop psychology" approach to love—basically, self-help books written by authors with varied credentials. Another involves serious psychological attempts to understand love and its antecedents. In this chapter, I review some of the earlier approaches through psychology (see also Sternberg, 1987, upon which the remainder of this chapter partially draws).

Literature helps us understand not only love but also the forces that can undermine and even destroy love: family quarrels, economic hardship, incompatible goals in life, jealousy, inability to control one's rage or other negative emotions, and so forth. When it comes to love, many of us, like Othello, are our own worst enemies. Seeing parts of ourselves in others through literature can help us learn not only what we should do in order to make love succeed, but also what we should not do.

Many of the early Greek and Roman myths were about love. Some were about love between mortals, some about love between gods, and some about love between mortals and gods. These myths often emphasized the role of fate. Fate may indeed play a role in love. But you will learn in this book that, to a surprising extent, when it comes to love, we have a considerable amount of control over our own destiny.

Early Psychological Approaches

Reinforcement Theories. One of the earliest approaches toward understanding the antecedents of love was based on reinforcement theories, which are theories aimed at explaining behavior through patterns of environmental rewards (as well as punishments). Al and Bernice Lott (1961, 1974) believed that attraction, an antecedent to love, results when a person whom one initially likes either is positively reinforcing or happens to be present when reinforcements are provided. In other words, one can come to be attracted to someone either because the person is rewarding or because one happens to experience rewards in the presence of that person. That is why when you go out on a date with someone in whom you are interested, you pick a romantic setting: You hope that the rewarding characteristics of the setting will enhance the potential partner's positive feelings toward you. Based on this view, perhaps John and Jane, mentioned at the beginning of the chapter, failed to do enough "fun stuff" together, and as a result the attraction wore off.

Jerry Clore and Donn Byrne (1974) proposed a related model. Their model essentially claims that one's attraction to someone depends on the ratio of positive reinforcements experienced with the person to the total number of reinforcements. In other words, what matters is not only the positive experiences of an individual but also the number of negative experiences. So it is great if you have a lot of positive experiences with your partner, but if you have too many negative experiences as well, the reward value of the positive experiences may be diminished. People often tire of spouses who are inconsistent—very kind one day, and mean and inconsiderate the next. The negative experiences can predominate over the positive ones, even when, numerically, there are more positive ones.

A follow-up on such work was proposed by George Homans (1974). Homans suggested that people seek to maximize rewards and minimize punishments. But he further pointed out that, after a certain point, people experience diminishing returns—that is, repeated positive rewards lose their effectiveness over time, as do repeated punishments. So, for example, if you like to give your partner jewelry as a reward, you will need to keep finding nicer and nicer pieces in order to avoid diminishing returns, or you may choose to find some other kind of present so that the reward value of your presents does not diminish.

Elaine Walster, G. W. Walster, and Ellen Berscheid (1978) went a giant step further when they proposed what came to be called equity theory. According to this theory, there are four principles for establishing equity in a relationship. First, as noted by previous theorists, individuals seek to maximize their outcomes (rewards minus punishments). Second, a couple can maximize their collective reward by developing a system they agree upon for equitably apportioning rewards and costs between themselves. A couple, for example, can decide that one partner will do more of the housework and the other partner more of the child care. But if one partner does almost all of the housework and all of the child care, that partner may feel deprived of an equitable relationship. Third, partners who find themselves in what they consider to be an inequitable relationship become distressed, and the more inequitable the relationship, the more distress they experience. Finally, the more an individual feels deprived of equity, the harder he or she will work to establish or reestablish equity. In other words, if you are in an inequitable relationship, the relationship bears a resemblance to a time bomb. The longer the relationship remains inequitable, the more potentially explosive it becomes as frustration builds in the partner who feels inequitably treated. If both partners feel unfairly treated, then the relationship is truly at risk.

Equity theory went beyond mere reinforcement principles. It proved to be something of a transition between traditional reinforcement theories and a subsequent type called cognitive-consistency theories.

Cognitive-Consistency Theories. Cognitive-consistency theories basically hold that people strive to keep their cognitions psychologically consistent. When their cognitions become inconsistent, people try to restore consistency. For example, if a woman feels that her spouse treats her well but learns that he is cruel toward his colleagues at work, whom she likes, she may consider these two pieces of knowledge inconsistent and try to restore some measure of consistency—for example, either through deciding that perhaps her spouse is not so nice to her after all or through deciding that in fact her spouse could not possibly be cruel toward others and that therefore she have been misinformed.

Fritz Heider (1958) proposed what he called balance theory, according to which relationships can be represented by triangles that relate people and feelings about people. Consider, for example, the situation described above. A woman has a positive relationship with her husband but learns that he has a negative relationship with colleagues at work. There are three relationships here: the woman with the husband, the woman with the colleagues at work, and the husband with the colleagues at work. Two of the relationships are positive (the woman with the husband and the woman with the husband's colleagues at work) and one is negative (the husband with his colleagues at work). According to Heider, the presence of an odd number of negatives—that is, either one or three in this case—creates an unbalanced triangle. According to Heider, to balance the triangle with one negative, the woman is likely either to come to view her husband more negatively or to come to view his colleagues at work more negatively. Either way, she can balance the triangle by creating two negatives rather than one.

According to Heider, a triangle with three negatives is also unbalanced. If X, Y, and Z all feel negatively toward each other, it is likely that either X and Y, Y and Z, or X and Z will become allies against the third. (There is an old saying, "My enemy's enemy is my friend," which can be understood in terms of Heider's balance theory.) For example, the current situation among Israel, Hamas, and the Palestinian authority—where all are fighting with each other—represents an unbalanced triangle, and for this reason one would expect either the two Palestinian organizations eventually to ally with each other or the Israelis to ally with one or the other group.

An interesting implication of cognitive-consistency theory is that if a person comes to cause injury to another for any reason other than dislike, the person may actually come to feel negatively toward that other person simply to create cognitive consistency. If someone treats you poorly, therefore, the more you highlight to the person how poorly he or she is treating you, the more likely that person is to become antagonistic toward you, even if he or she was not initially antagonistic (e.g., if the other person treated you negatively but in a way that he or she viewed as purely a matter of business competition).

Clinical Approaches

Early clinical approaches took a stance quite different from the more social–psychological approaches described above.

For example, Sigmund Freud (1955/1922) viewed love in terms of sublimated sexuality. We are limited by societal conventions in our sexual possibilities with others. So we come to love them as a way of trying, in essence, to put our sexual feelings on a higher plane. Jim may be desperate to have sex with his neighbor's wife, Jill, but the impossibility of the situation may cause him to have feelings of love toward her. Of course, Freud lived in Victorian times. Today Jim may try to have sex with her and possibly even skip the love part.

Theodore Reik (1944) viewed love in a different way. He believed that it arose out of feelings of dissatisfaction with both oneself and one's life. We love as a way of finding happiness in the face of multiple dissatisfactions with how things have worked out for us.

Abraham Maslow (1954) suggested that there are actually two rather distinct kinds of love: what he referred to as D-love and B-love. D-love is deficiency love, which arises out of people's needs for security and belongingness—in other words, out of deficiencies we find in ourselves. Through the lover, we are trying to compensate for what we find inadequate in ourselves. Maslow viewed this form of love as inferior to B-love, or being love. B-love is the love that comes out of people's desire to self-actualize, that is, to fulfill themselves as human beings. In reality, most loves probably represent some combination of the two.

Dorothy Tennov (1979) proposed that people differ in a key way in what she called limerence, or the tendency to fall madly in love with another. People who are susceptible to limerence tend to find themselves acutely longing for someone else, to be completely absorbed by that person, and to have trouble getting the person out of their thoughts. People who are not limerent do not experience these feelings and often do not understand them in people who do.

WHEN IS IT LOVE?

The question I am asked most often is some variant of: "When is it love? I know I like _____, but I'm not sure I love him (her)." The theories described in this chapter and especially later in the book may help you answer this question for yourself. But first it may help to think about the relation between liking and loving. This may seem to be simple, but it's anything but.

One view is that love is what happens when you like someone a whole lot. I will argue later that there is in fact a condition characterized by extremely high levels of intimacy that constitutes love. But generally, and for most people, love is more than extreme liking. Indeed, you may find yourself liking someone you date very much and wonder why you can't fall in love with him (or her). Or you may find, even more annoyingly, that you love someone you don't even like much. Loving does not seem to be equivalent to just a lot of liking.

A second view is that liking is the next step after loving—that loving may indeed be something very different from liking, but it follows from liking. Sometimes this is the case, but certainly not always. Sometimes we fall in love with someone before we even have gotten to know the person very well. We can hardly say we like that person, because we scarcely know him (or her). And sometimes the loving just never follows, no matter how hard we try. Loving may follow liking, but then it may not.

A third view is that liking and loving have really very little to do with each other—that they are related but distinct constructs. On one hand, this can be true—for example, if we find ourselves loving someone but not liking him (or her). On the other hand, most of the time we do like the people we love. So liking seems usually, but not always, to accompany loving.

A fourth view is that liking and loving are essentially overlapping constructs—that liking usually, although not always, constitutes a part of loving, but loving does not typically constitute a part of liking. This is the view that I will take in this book. Liking and loving are not the same. But if we love someone without liking that person, we probably have a problem. We may be in a relationship that is no longer working, or that was doomed from the start.

WHY IS LOVE IMPORTANT ANYWAY?

With all these different theories of love floating around, one might well ask: Why is love so important anyway? Why do philosophers, writers, psychologists, and others devote so much time and effort to trying to understand this phenomenon? Before closing the chapter, let's consider why love is important not only to these people, but to you as well.

First, as you will see later in the book, love has great evolutionary significance. It provides one of the key means by which humans propagate their species. However love may benefit its experiencers, it is especially beneficial to those who are born as a result of it. Moreover, it is the love of the child by the parents that often will keep those parents together and thus provide the nurturant environment infants and children need in order to develop into responsible and happy adults.

Second, the value of love in keeping couples together is important not only to the children, but to the couple as well. People who stay together, usually through marriage, tend to have happier, more satisfying lives than do people whose attempts to find partners repeatedly lead to failure and breakups. That said, there are many people who find happiness living alone or with serial partners, never fully committing to another person.

Third, in most societies, it is economically beneficial for couples to stay together. So love helps to provide a stable economic as well as social life. People who break up repeatedly end up with financial burdens that people who stay together are often (but certainly not always) able to avoid.

Fourth, many people find, as they grow older, that however important love may have been to them when they were younger, it becomes what is most important when they are older. Careers can be challenging and rewarding while people have them, but most people who survive long enough eventually retire. When they retire, they may find, somewhat to their surprise, that their former colleagues quickly leave them behind. The work into which they put so much effort seems to become part of the distant past. In many occupations, one's accomplishments rather quickly become passé or are even undone after the person retires. A loving spouse and family can be what provides most of the happiness in life as one becomes older and one's world revolves more and more around family and no longer around work.

Because love is important to us and, if anything, increases in importance as we get older, we need to understand what it is—and what it is not. As a psychologist, I have found my understanding of love invaluable in figuring out my own relationships. I have been in relationships where the characteristics of my interaction with another person seemed to stray from what I knew about love from my studies of psychology. These relationships invariably failed. And when I finally found the relationship of my dreams, I was reassured to find that it so closely resembled what not only one, but several psychologists had found to characterize relationships that succeed not only in the short term, but over the course of one's entire life.

In this book, you will learn all about love and its facets. Reading the book will be a great adventure. Enjoy that adventure, and profit from it in your own life. Don't end up the way John and Jane did!

Love From a Biological Perspective

Quite a few theories have been proposed to account for love from a biological perspective, but they all have a common root: In 1859 Charles Darwin published a book called *The Origin of Species*, which is widely considered the basis for evolutionary biology. In his book Darwin suggested that species evolve and develop over generations through a process called natural selection. Humans, just like animals, plants, and other organisms, need to reproduce so that they can pass on their genes to the next generation. But passing on one's genes isn't as easy as it may sound. People have always faced situations and problems that challenge their survival and reproduction. The actual problems have changed over time and include finding food to enable oneself and one's family to survive, finding a partner with whom to have a family, protecting one's children from predators, and many more. Of the ways in which people have responded to the problems they encountered, some have been more adaptive than others. Darwin suggested that, ultimately, those traits and features that evolved over many generations were the most adaptive and were best suited to help people survive and reproduce. Almost any feature you encounter today in human physiology and behavior has its roots in our ancient history and in productive responses to the challenges our species once faced and, in some cases, continues to face. Males and females sometimes differ in the ways they face these challenges. For example, males, on average, evaluate potential mates differently than females. Males tend to place greater emphasis on female physical attractiveness as a proxy for reproductive capacity, and females tend to place more emphasis on the resource-gathering abilities of males.

Adaptive traits are helpful to a species in two ways. First, they can enhance the survival of individuals and their families. A strong male, for example, will be better able than a weak one to fend off enemies and threats or to hunt large animals, illustrating the concept of "survival of the fittest." Second, adaptive traits help an individual to successfully reproduce and pass his or her genes on to the next generation, a phenomenon called sexual selection. A good example of sexual selection is the mane of a lion. It does not help a male lion to physically survive in the savannah. What it does, however, is attract female lions so that the male can mate with them and have as many viable offspring as possible.

The features that help species survive and reproduce are commonly of a physical nature, but they also can be psychological. Evolutionary psychology explores those mechanisms. It first gained prominence in the early 1980s. Today there are a number of evolution-based theories that are intended to explain love from a biological perspective, and we'll take a closer look at some of them in this chapter. First, we will consider the evolution of sexual preferences. We will then turn to a view of love as involving decision-making biases. Next, we will look at love from an attachment perspective. Finally, we will consider what happens in the brain when someone is in love.

EVOLUTION OF SEXUAL PREFERENCES

According to David Buss, love developed to serve the following functions (Buss, 1988, 2006, p. 66):

- Displaying reproductively relevant resources
- Providing sexual access
- Signaling sexual fidelity
- Promoting relationship exclusivity through mate guarding
- Displaying commitment
- Promoting actions that lead to successful reproductive outcomes
- Providing signals of parental investment

Love is hypothesized to assist humans in several ways. First, when you're in love with someone, it gives you an opportunity to have sexual intercourse with that person and eventually to have children to pass on your genes. But when you show your love to your partner, in our society you also signal that you are committed to your relationship and won't engage in a relationship with someone else at the same time. When the two of you have children, showing love also indicates that you are committed to caring for your children. Because love evolved over such a long time in human history, evolutionary theory suggests that it is something that is shared by all human beings, no matter where they live or what culture they belong to. Not everyone is hypothesized to experience love in exactly the same way, however. Love can be shaped by factors such as gender, age, and culture. The point is that every normally functioning human being has a propensity to experience love at some point in his or her life.

In the 19th century, certain groups viewed romantic love as an undesirable emotion (either because they thought it was too lustful or because they saw it as just plain disruptive to the achievement of community goals), and so they tried to ban love. Such groups included the Oneida Society and the Shakers. However, it proved impossible to eliminate love in these groups. Love persisted despite all regulations, and where it was forbidden, lovers merely retreated underground. A study asking people in a variety of countries whether they were currently in love found that more than half of the respondents were in love at the time, further suggesting that love is a universal emotion (Sprecher et al., 1994).

Although love appears to be universal, men and women tend to experience it differently. You may have noticed some of these differences in your everyday life. Think about it. What are the attributes you believe a desirable partner should have? Do you think members of the opposite gender have the same preferences and priorities, or do their preferences differ from yours? Whatever preferences you come up with, it is not unlikely that you have identified some gender differences.

As noted above, physical appearance tends to be more important to men than it is to women. From an evolutionary standpoint, this trend makes good sense. Men want to increase the chances that sexual intercourse with a woman will lead to conception, and the chances are greater the younger and healthier the woman is. Outward cues for health and youth in women include long hair, symmetrical features, smooth skin, and large breasts (Sugiyama, 2005; see also Stone, Shackelford, & Buss, 2008).

Women face a different problem. They have to invest 9 months in each pregnancy and will likely be the ones primarily to raise their offspring. Moreover, the years in which they can reproduce are fairly limited. In contrast, men can father children up to old age and also can father children at a much higher rate: There is no 9-month wait for them! So, generally, it is more important to women that the father of their children have high status or the potential to attain it, ambition, and industriousness, because these attributes suggest that he will be able to provide her and their children with the resources they need to thrive (Buss, 2006).

Of course, physical appearance can matter to women too; it just is not as important, on average, to women as it is to men. However, physical appearance is more important to women when they are looking for a short-term partner than when they are looking for a man with whom they hope to build a family at some point (Gangestad & Thornhill, 1997; Sugiyama, 2005).

As a result of human evolution, ovulation in women takes place in relatively concealed conditions. In particular, there is no way a man can look at a woman and know for sure whether she is ready to conceive. So in hopes of ensuring conception with a particular woman, a man typically will have to stay with her for some length of time. Perhaps for this reason (as well as others), men and women started to have sexual intercourse on a continuous basis and to stay together for longer periods of time, if not a lifetime. Thus, women often dedicate their entire reproductive life span to one partner while men invest relatively heavily in their children. But when people choose a partner for reasons such as beauty or wealth, at some point in their lives it will seem to make sense to choose another partner. So what is it that will reassure partners that a mate will be with them in good as well as bad times? This is where evolutionary psychologists believe love comes into the picture. By being loved, people can be (relatively) confident that their partner will stay with and care for them even if they get sick or face some other misfortune, or if a more attractive potential mate comes along. And, of course, the feeling of being in love is a reward in itself and has often been compared to feelings of addiction.

CHAPTER 2

EXCURSION: SEXUAL ORIENTATION

When we talk about romantic love in this book, we usually refer to heterosexual love, that is, the love between a man and a woman. However, the book would not be complete without at least a short review of some of the latest research on homosexuality. There always has been a great deal of controversy around the topic. It was only in 1986 that homosexuality was completely removed from the revised version of the *Diagnostic and Statistical Manual of Mental Disorders (DSM-III)*, which is a manual that psychiatrists and psychologists use to diagnose psychological disorders. As of this printing, nine states in the United States allow same-sex marriages, and gay rights are still a topic of vivid discussion all around the country and the world. Let us have a look at what research can tell us about sexual orientation. Is it genetic or not, and can it really be changed, as some people and institutions claim?

If you want to find out whether a behavior has a genetic foundation, there are three ways you can go about your endeavor. First, you can do a family study and investigate whether homosexuality runs in families. Second, you can conduct a twin study and see whether there is a difference in rates of homosexuality between monozygotic (identical) and dizygotic (fraternal) twins who grew up in the same household. And third, you can employ the research methods of molecular genetics (Mustanski & Bailey, 2003).

Family studies have found that homosexuality indeed tends to run in families. That is, the chances that a gay male has a gay brother or that a lesbian has a lesbian sister are higher than the chances for a heterosexual person to have a homosexual brother or sister (Mustanski, Chivers, & Bailey, 2002). This fact supports the hypothesis that there may be some genetic influence at play.

However, it is not definitive; similar environments might contribute to the effect, or be the entire cause of it. If indeed genes are involved, what is not quite clear is whether the same gene plays a role for men and women, or if separate genes influence male and female sexual orientation. Obviously, if there is one gene for both men and women, then families in which homosexuality occurs should have both gay and lesbian family members. If there are different genes for male and female sexual orientations, then either male or female homosexuality, and not necessarily both, should run in families. Studies on this topic so far have found no conclusive evidence as to which assumption is true (Mustanski & Bailey, 2003).

Researchers who accept the genetic hypothesis believe it is most likely that a gene responsible for sexual orientation is located on the X chromosome. This is because the Y chromosome is small and does not contain much information, at least relative to the X chromosome. Since men get their X chromosome from their mothers, it is hypothesized that male homosexuality must be transmitted from the maternal side. If that is the case, then gay men should have a higher percentage of gay relatives on the maternal side of their family than on the paternal side. Studies investigating this conjecture have not found conclusive evidence to confirm or disconfirm it (see for example McKnight & Malcolm, 2000).

Twin studies have found that there seems to be a heritability of .62 for sexual orientation in both genders (Kendler, Thornton, Gilman, & Kessler, 2000), which suggests that genes do indeed play a role. (Heritability is the proportion of phenotypic, or observable variable, properties due to genetic effects.) Other influences, such as experiences in early childhood, may have an impact as well. One region on the X chromosome has been identified that may influence male sexual orientation (Hamer, Hu, Magnuson, & Pattatucci, 1993).

CHAPTER 2

LOVE AS DECISION-MAKING BIASES

As we've already learned, some tendencies in human behavior have evolved over history to help our species survive and reproduce. How do those tendencies translate into behavior that we label "love"? How do they influence which individuals we feel attracted to and how we try to maintain our relationship with a partner or care for our family? Douglas Kenrick (2006) has suggested that when we make decisions in the domain of love, these decisions are influenced by biases that have developed throughout human history. When it comes right down to it, these decision biases are just what they sound like: cold, economic rules that are meant to further the survival of the species. This doesn't sound much like a theory of love, does it? It certainly isn't a rose-colored perspective on love, but neither is the age-old struggle for survival that humans and all other living beings face every day.

This approach assumes that the human mind is made up of a complex system of biases that guide the decisions we have to make in daily life. So any tendencies you have to behave in a certain way in a given situation may result from these decision biases. The goal of these biases is, as we've discussed, to increase the chances that an individual survives and passes his or her genes on to another generation. The decision biases are different for men and for women because each gender faces different challenges, and women have to invest much more in their offspring than men necessarily have to (Geary, 1998; Trivers, 1972). Furthermore, there are many different decision biases. What they have in common, though, is that they are essentially predispositions that make you pay more attention to some particular features of your environment than to others and cause you to react with certain emotions to those features.

Most people are engaged in a number of different intimate relationships at any point in their lives. Think about the different intimate relationships you have had—with your parents, your siblings, and the friends who have attended college with you; perhaps you are in a romantic relationship with someone as well. Although these are all intimate relationships in which love may be involved, the problems and issues you encounter differ from one relationship to another. So it makes sense that there would be different mechanisms in your mind to guide you in the decisions you have to make. For example, one relationship might involve questions regarding faithfulness, another questions involving financial resources, and still another questions involving both.

Another thing that makes decision biases really effective is that they are dynamic. That is, they interact with those of other people. This interaction happens in the form of "if/then" rules. The behavior option you choose, therefore, depends not only on your own internal decision biases, but also on the input you receive from other people. Culture has an impact on the decision rules surrounding love, but that impact is limited because our decision biases have developed over human evolution based on the problems our ancestors faced.

So how do these rules translate into everyday life? Think about your own preferences first. When meeting people who could be potential partners, what do you look for first? If you are a man, there is a good chance you pay more attention to physical beauty and youth, whereas if you are a woman, you are likely to pay more attention to a man's status. According to Kenrick, this is because youth and beauty may indicate the reproductive qualities of a potential partner, which are important for men, who do not have to invest a lot of effort into having offspring. Men should be most interested in the continuation of their gene pool. Women, on the other hand, have to invest a lot in their offspring and therefore have to be sure that the father of their children will be able to provide for them as best as possible. Once you are together with a partner, you are likely to be hypervigilant toward any potential interloper or any behavior that may indicate that your partner is unfaithful to you. This hypervigilance makes sense from an evolutionary perspective because a male wants to ensure that his partner does not have offspring that, unbeknownst to him, are of a different father; and a female wants to be confident that she has the continued support of the father in raising her children.

A different level of significance applies to your family and to other people to whom you are genetically related. In general, one wants the family members who share one's gene pool to survive as best as possible. Therefore, it is essential to support them and to maintain reasonably good relationships with them. In such a family relationship, you may pay less attention to inequities than you do in other relationships, and you probably also pay considerable attention to your children's needs (as opposed to the needs of those who are not part of your core family).

There is some empirical support for Kenrick's assertions. In one study, people in groups played a game of trivia and then were told that their team had done quite well. When they had played with strangers on their team, they attributed most of their team's success to themselves; when they had played with family members on their team, however, they attributed more of their team's success to those family members (Ackerman, Ledlow, & Kenrick, 2003). Studies also have shown that we tend to be more generous with family members than with strangers (e.g., Ledlow & Linder, 2003).

LOVE FROM AN ATTACHMENT PERSPECTIVE

A very different biological approach to explaining love has its roots in John Bowlby's attachment theory (1969/1982, 1980). Before we move on to adult attachment and love, however, let us review the origins and nature of attachment theory.

Bowlby observed what you surely have seen many times and may even have taken for granted: Infants seek proximity with their caregivers. Bowlby wondered why they seek it. Is it just because their caregivers feed them and keep them warm? He argued that this is not the case, but rather that human infants are actually "pre-programmed" to establish an attachment with their caregivers because this attachment helps them survive. However, all parents and other caregivers do not react in the same way to babies' or children's efforts to communicate their needs and to establish a close bond, and the way they do react can affect the kind of attachment the child forms with the parent or other caregiver.

A child's attachment to parents can take different forms. The form depends on the feedback the child receives, the speed with which the feedback is given, and whether the parent or other caregiver can offer the child food and comfort. In general, Bowlby proposed the existence of three distinct attachment styles: secure, avoidant, and anxious/ambivalent.

A secure attachment style leads infants generally to be comfortable in their relationship with their caregivers and to be tolerant when caregivers leave temporarily. They use the caregiver as a safe base from which to explore the world. A securely attached infant prefers the caregivers over strangers.

An avoidant infant does not show a marked preference for the caregiver over a stranger. Moreover, the avoidant infant does not react strongly when the caregiver leaves or returns.

An anxiously attached infant reacts very strongly when the caregiver leaves and is afraid to be left alone. The infant is very reactive and tries hard to get closer to the caregiver. Yet the anxious child also shows a certain ambivalence to the caregiver and feels insecurely attached.

Shaver, Hazan, and Bradshaw (1988) used Bowlby's theory as a basis to think about adult relationships and adult attachment. They suggested that the same principles that apply to infants also

TABLE 2.1 **ADULT ATTACHMENT TYPES**

Choose which of the following three styles best describes your relationships with others.
1. You like being close to others and find it easy to establish closeness. You're not afraid of someone getting too close to you or someone abandoning you. You don't mind depending on others or if others depend on you.
2. You feel uneasy at times when others are close to you, and you don't like to depend on others. You find it hard to trust others. Often, your romantic partners try to get closer to you than you would like.
3. You feel that others often don't like as much closeness as you do. Your desire for closeness makes others shy away from you at times. You find yourself worrying that your partner will abandon you or doesn't love you.

Source: Based on Hazan and Shaver (1987).

apply to adult romantic relationships. In adult intimate relationships, you also can find touching, caressing, eye contact, and smiling. Furthermore, a secure relationship can be formed only when the partner is available and responsive to one's needs.

Before we go on to discuss some more details of this approach, you may be interested in finding out about your own attachment style with respect to romantic love. Hazan and Shaver (1987) developed descriptions of the three attachment styles that you can use to find where your style fits best (Table 2.1). Other instruments have been developed more recently that measure attachment style on a continuous scale or that have added a second type of avoidance: dismissing–avoidance (e.g., Bartholomew & Horowitz, 1991; Fraley, Waller, & Brennan, 2000). Obviously, there's no shortage of scales. But the one by Hazan and Shaver (1987) gives a handy overview of the three original styles.

Have you decided which of the three descriptions in Table 2.1 best reflects your feelings? The first option describes a secure attachment style, the second an avoidant attachment style, and the third an anxious/ambivalent attachment style. When

Hazan and Shaver first published their scale in a newspaper and asked readers to answer the questions and submit their answers to the researchers, 56% of the participants categorized themselves as securely attached, 25% described themselves as avoidant, and 19% described themselves as anxiously attached. People who thought of themselves as securely attached spoke of their relationships as warm and supportive and believed that relationships can be maintained over a long period of time. Anxiously attached people experienced a lot of passion and even obsession with their partners, but showed a tendency to be jealous and to feel their partners were untrustworthy. And people with an avoidant style thought the interactions with their partners were not always friendly and that emotional involvement was relatively low. They also believed that love cannot be maintained over a long period of time (Hazan & Shaver, 1987). A recent study that assessed how young adults were attached to their partners found that a secure attachment style correlates positively with compassionate love (involving mutual respect, trust, and affection) for their partners, whereas an anxious-dismissive style correlates negatively with compassionate love. An anxious attachment style is neither positively nor negatively correlated with compassionate love (Sprecher & Fehr, 2011).

Bowlby (1969/1982) postulated that there are three different behavioral systems: an attachment system, a caregiving system, and a sexual system. The attachment system serves to protect a person from danger by keeping her close to others who care about her. The caregiving system provides protection to others. And the sexual system is designed to ensure that a person can pass on his genes to the next generation. Cognitive-behavioral mechanisms monitor our progress toward achieving the goals of each system.

We start out with a primary strategy for achieving our goal. If necessary, we then alter our behavior to improve our chances of reaching our goal. Over time, our actions adjust to our social environment and to our partners to be maximally effective. This is how we acquire a particular style of attachment. The strategies that we adjust can be either hyperactivating or deactivating. Hyperactivating strategies correspond to an anxiously attached style and deactivating strategies correspond to an avoidant style.

For example, because the goal of the attachment system is to keep one safe, the primary strategy in this system is to seek proximity to one's partner. If the partner is not readily available, one may try out other strategies to feel safe and achieve proximity with one's beloved. The hyperactivating strategy is characterized by strong demands for the partner's attention and hypervigilance toward any behavior that could be interpreted as a sign of rejection. The deactivating strategy may involve avoidance of closeness with the partner and exaggerated self-reliance. Do you recognize how the anxious and avoidant styles are demonstrated in those two strategies? According to Shaver, over time people tend to display an adult attachment style that is closely related to their attachment style in early childhood (Ainsworth, 1989; Shaver & Mikulincer, 2006).

Consider the relationship of Alex and Rose. Alex has always had an intense desire to be very close to Rose, both physically and emotionally. He wants to share everything in his life and be with Rose as much as possible. In the beginning of their relationship, Rose responded to his needs and wishes, and they were nearly inseparable. But as time went on, Rose felt an increasing need to have some alone time. Alex was almost suffocating her, she thought. So she started to withdraw and respond less to his attempts to be close to her. At the same time, Alex became more and more demanding, insisting they spend all their free time together and that she not spend any time with male friends. This led to Rose's withdrawing from him more and more until eventually they broke up.

In this relationship, Rose did not respond to Alex's needs in the way Alex expected, and so his primary strategy of seeking her company and closeness did not work well for him—or for her. He then resorted to a hyperactivating strategy reflecting his anxious attachment style and started crowding her. His fierce demands on her time drove her even further from him.

The goal of the caregiving system is a very altruistic one: to support and take care of another person. The primary strategy for this behavioral system is to be empathetic toward others and to engage in helping behaviors. This pattern also can be categorized under altruistic or compassionate love. Again, when people feel that their behavior is not helping them realize their intentions, they may resort to hyperactivating or deactivating strategies. Hyperactivating responses lead one to exaggerate the need of other people to be helped or to force assistance upon them, whereas deactivating strategies make one tend to ignore the needs and suffering of others or to seek distance from them when they need help.

The goal of the sexual system is to enable a person to pass his or her genes on to the next generation. The primary strategy here is to attract others sexually and to persuade them to engage in sexual intercourse. If the response diverges from the desired one, the hyperactivating strategy would be to attempt to force sexual intercourse on a partner and to be extremely sensitive to signs of sexual rejection. The deactivating strategy would include a denial of one's sexual needs or a lack of responsiveness to a partner who wants to engage in sexual activity.

The different strategies people employ to achieve the goals of the caregiving, attachment, and sexual systems are also useful tools for addressing dysfunctional relationships. People who employ hyperactivating strategies and have an anxious attachment style can feel chronically frustrated because they cannot get as close to their loved ones as they wish. They are very sensitive and tend to be jealous toward their partners. They also tend to worry excessively about their relationship (e.g., Simpson, Ickes, & Grich, 1999). People with an avoidant attachment style (employing deactivating strategies), in contrast, have trouble committing fully to their relationships and tend to withdraw (e.g., Collins & Read, 1990).

Research has shown that there are brain systems that seem to coincide with the different behavioral systems: The sexual system, which is responsible for the desire to engage in sexual activities with one or more partners, is associated with both estrogens and androgens. With respect to the androgens, testosterone is largely responsible for the sex drive, both in women and in men (Sherwin, 1994; Van Goozen, Wiegant, Endert, Helmond, & Van de Poll, 1997). As is often the case in biological psychology, functional magnetic resonance imaging (fMRI) studies have been conducted to identify which areas of the human brain are activated when a person feels a particular emotion or performs a specific task. When someone is sexually aroused, studies have found that a number of brain areas are activated, especially the hypothalamus and the amygdala (Beauregard, Levesque, & Bourgouin, 2001; Fonteille & Stoleru, 2011; Stoleru, Fonteille, Cornelis, Joyal, & Moulier, 2012).

The attachment system, which is responsible for behaviors such as seeking proximity to supportive persons and longing for a partner's attention, is associated with two hormones: oxytocin in the nucleus accumbens, also known as the pleasure center of the brain, and vasopressin in the ventral pallidum, a structure within the basal ganglia (Lim, Murphy, & Young, 2004; Lim & Young, 2004).

Attraction (or, you could say, romantic love) is often marked by strong passionate feelings and efforts to win over a desired mate. It is associated with increased levels of the neurotransmitters dopamine and norepinephrine, as well as with lower levels of serotonin (Acevedo, Arthur, Fisher, & Brown, 2012; Fisher, 1998, 2004).

The existence of these three separate brain systems makes it possible for us to experience a deep attachment to one person while we are romantically attracted to someone else. We can feel sexually aroused by someone to whom we do not feel attached or romantically attracted, for example, when reading a magazine or watching a movie that features very attractive people.

LOVE AND THE BRAIN

Romantic love starts with feeling attracted to someone and at the same time feeling that person is special to us. This is called mate preference, and it is exhibited not only by humans, but also by all other mammals and by birds. When we or other mammals or birds feel attracted to that special one, we all experience the same symptoms: We may feel sleepless and that our energy and attention are focused on our beloved one; we also may feel possessive and exhibit a lack of appetite. Animal studies have shown that mate preference is associated with raised levels of central dopamine.

Consider a prairie vole (raised in a lab) that is mating with a particular male. As she mates, the dopamine in her nucleus accumbens increases by a staggering 50% (Gingrich et al., 2000). However, when a dopamine antagonist is injected into her accumbens, she suddenly no longer prefers that male. If we could do this in humans, might we be on the way toward finding a cure for broken hearts?

From an evolutionary standpoint, we might ask why mate preference developed in the first place. Fisher (1998, 2004, 2006) suspects that by our preferring a specific individual, we are able to save courtship time and energy. And in human evolution, this mate preference at some point developed into what we now recognize as romantic love.

You may know some people who are very quick to fall in love, in contrast to others, who seem very deliberate and slow to fall in love. How easily people fall in love may be influenced by their genes. Our baseline levels of dopamine and serotonin are determined by specific genes, and because these neurotransmitters play a crucial role in the process of falling in love, they are responsible for individual differences in our readiness to fall in love (Fisher, 2006; Gibbons, 2004). Other factors also play a role in how easily we fall in love. Drug use and diseases such as schizophrenia and Parkinson's can change dopaminergic pathways. And even being in a novel situation with a member of the opposite sex can create romantic feelings, probably because the experience of novelty raises central dopamine activity (Fisher, 2004).

Fortunately, we don't all share the same mate preference. People differ widely in whom they find attractive and with whom they can imagine having a loving relationship. So what determines with whom we fall in love? A number of different factors come into play. First of all, a person must be ready to fall in love (Hatfield, 1988). Being physically close to a person also may create mutual attraction (Pines, 1999). Most people fall in love with others who are similar to them ethnically, socially, and with regard to educational and economic background, as well as with regard to attitudes and interests (Buston & Emlen, 2003; Pines, 1999). Biological processes have an impact as well. Women are especially attracted to men who differ from them in the characteristics of their immune system (Wedekind et al., 1995). It is not clear, however, if all of these stimuli trigger a response in the brain or if it is actually the chemical processes in the brain that influence someone's interest in a particular individual.

So what exactly goes on in our brains when we are in love? We have already taken a short look at the three different brain systems. Now we will go into some more detail. Helen Fisher and her colleagues (Fisher et al., 2003, 2005) conducted a study in which the participants were people who had recently fallen in love. The participants were shown photos of their romantic partners and of acquaintances toward whom they had no particularly positive or negative feelings. In between showings of the photos, they were given a distracting task. They were asked to count down in increments of 7 from some large number. This task served to neutralize any strong emotions they might be feeling. While the participants were looking at the photos and performing the counting task, fMRI was used to record the activity in their brains. The expectation of the researchers was that participants would show elevated activity of central dopamine and/or norepinephrine, as well as lowered activity of central serotonin. These expectations were confirmed, especially for dopamine: When participants looked at the photos of their partners, several brain areas became activated, the most important of which were the right ventral tegmental area (VTA) and the right posterodorsal body and dorsal tail of the caudate nucleus. The VTA contains a lot of dopamine-producing cells. Some of that dopamine is distributed to the caudate nucleus. Furthermore, the VTA is part of the brain's reward system and is associated with feelings of pleasure, arousal, and motivation. The caudate nucleus is associated with motivation as well, and it is also involved in goal-oriented behavior. These brain areas were also found to be involved through studies that used as participants people who had been in love much longer—more than 2 years on average (Bartels & Zeki, 2000, 2004; see also Acevedo et al., 2012). This result indicates that dopamine is likely to be involved in those aspects of romantic love that involve motivation and goal-oriented behavior. We know that dopamine also can be associated with sensations such as ecstasy, sleeplessness, and craving (Fisher, 1998), so it probably plays a role when we experience these feelings while in love as well.

Furthermore, Fisher (1998, 2004; see also Acevedo et al., 2012) has hypothesized that norepinephrine and serotonin also may be involved when we are in love. An elevated activity of norepinephrine can lead to symptoms such as a pounding heart and elevated blood pressure, both of which are associated with being in love. Another study looked at both lovers and people with obsessive-compulsive disorder (Marazziti, Akiskal, Rossi, & Cassano, 1999) and found that both groups, in comparison with healthy people who were not in love, exhibited lower levels of the platelet serotonin transporter. As you may know or may have even experienced yourself, someone who is in love may think obsessively about their loved one, so the comparison of lovers with patients suffering from obsessive-compulsive disorder makes a great deal of sense. In both cases, lower serotonin activation may contribute to the experience of obsession.

As many of us have found, at some point in a relationship the obsession and excitement start to wear off. This is probably a good thing. Romantic love demands a lot from our metabolism and is costly to maintain in its early stages. It developed mainly to help us concentrate on winning the attention of a desired partner and is designed to last long enough for the relationship to bear offspring. Later, this elevated state often subsides and feelings of attachment come to the foreground. These feelings help to provide children with calmer and stabler conditions in which to grow up.

In sum, biological factors play an important role in love. Indeed, evolutionary psychologists argue that love evolved so that we can pass on our genes to subsequent generations. In order fully to understand love, we need to understand its biological antecedents as well as the brain-based mechanisms associated with it. But a full understanding of love also requires an understanding of the social–psychological factors that contribute to love. These factors are considered in the next chapter.

Are There Different Kinds of Love? Taxonomic Approaches

When Joe was recently asked about the people he loves, the first person who came to mind was his wife, Melissa, who had been his high school sweetheart. Joe and Melissa also went to college together and have recently gotten married. Though the fiery passion of their high school romance has given way to more stable and secure feelings of love as they have settled into their life together, Joe has felt very fulfilled and committed in his relationship to Melissa.

Almost at the same time Joe thought of Melissa, he thought about his 9-month-old son, Sean. Joe loves Sean with a passion he would not have thought possible before he became a father. He gets excited every time he thinks about his son, misses him terribly when they are apart, and feels fiercely protective of him.

Then, of course, there are Joe's parents, toward whom he has very warm and trusting feelings, although not so much of a passionate love. Joe also feels some love and commitment toward his grandparents and other relatives. Outside the family, he thinks of his best friend, Paul, whom he has known since kindergarten and to whom he feels very close. Although Paul now lives far away and has been at a distance for a while, Joe and Paul have kept in relatively close contact. Paul is one of only a few people with whom Joe feels he can talk about everything.

Take a moment and think about the different relationships you have with the people in your life. Whom do you love? Is it a long list or a short list of people? And does the love you feel have the same characteristics for everyone on your list, or can love actually feel very different depending on whom you think about?

People describe many different relationships with the word "love" despite the differences among these relationships. It is for this reason that many researchers believe there are different kinds of love. But what and how many kinds of love are there? And how could we possibly measure them? These are some of the questions we will examine in this chapter.

Many of the theories described in this chapter involve taxonomies. But what exactly is a taxonomy? A taxonomy classifies observed phenomena on the basis of shared characteristics. Most taxonomies of love begin in the same place: The language of love is examined, whether through an examination of film, literature, music, or firsthand accounts of people about their love life. The researcher sorts through all those accounts, examining similarities to determine what the commonalities (and also differences) are among those descriptions of love. A number of different techniques then can be used to sort the data (Berscheid, 1985, 2006b). As you will see throughout this chapter, some of the types of love listed in one taxonomy also appear in other taxonomies. But some types of love are unique to a particular taxonomy.

We will start our tour of different love taxonomies with one from Clyde and Susan Hendrick, who have based their taxonomy on the "colors of love" theory by John Alan Lee. Then we will look at Robert Sternberg's duplex theory of love, which consists of a triangular taxonomy of different kinds of love and a theory of love as a story. Next we will consider Margaret Clark's suggestion that love results from communal responsiveness. And finally, we will consider Ellen Berscheid's proposal that there are four different kinds of love. Her taxonomy can help us describe love relationships as they change over the course of time.

LEE'S AND THE HENDRICKS' THEORY OF STYLES OF ROMANTIC LOVE

One of the earliest approaches to systematizing different kinds of love was undertaken by John Alan Lee (1973, 1988). First, Lee intensively and extensively analyzed the existing romantic literature, with the objects of examination ranging from poems to philosophical writings to research from the social sciences. To provide empirical support for his theory, he developed a method called the Love Story Card Sort. He presented his subjects with about 170 phrases like "The night after I met X. . . ." They then had to choose an answer from among 6 through 15 alternative responses (e.g., "I could hardly sleep after meeting X").

After analyzing his data, Lee suggested that there are three primary love styles (which he likened to primary colors) that represent "pure" styles, and three secondary love styles that represent mixtures of the three primary styles (which Lee likened to secondary colors, which are mixtures of the primary colors).

CHAPTER 3

Lee gave the love styles Greek and Latin names to correspond to terms used in classical literature. According to Lee's theory, everybody has a preference for a particular love style, but the love style a person exhibits depends also on the loved one. Love styles also may change as we grow older.

The three primary love styles are eros, storge, and ludus. *Eros* is a passionate kind of love that is characterized by strong emotions and intense physical longing for the loved one. It is what we are likely to think of when we think about romantic love. This kind of love has been featured in movies such as *Pretty Woman* (in which a prostitute falls in love with a wealthy businessman) and *Titanic* (in which a girl from a well-to-do family falls in love with a drifter).

Storge is a friendship-based love. It develops slowly out of friendship. With storge, should the lovers break up, there is a greater chance than with other love styles that they remain friends. In this love style, lovers place great emphasis on commitment in their relationship. Their love typically is not characterized by passionate emotions as in eros. The movie *When Harry Met Sally* (which follows Harry and Sally through 12 years of their lives, in which they keep meeting each other and build up a friendship that, by the end of the movie, results in romantic attraction) represents a good example of storge.

Ludus is also called game-playing love. It commonly is displayed by people who prefer to remain single and who see love as a game of conquest and numbers. Such lovers do not passionately fall in love with their chosen ones. Moreover, they recover quickly from a breakup when the "game" is over. They are more likely to display infidelity than people whose love style is storge or eros. Ludus is illustrated by the movie *Cruel Intentions* (in which stepsiblings seduce partners as part of a bet and to get even with others).

As noted above, the secondary love styles are made up of combinations of the three primary love styles. The secondary love styles are mania, pragma, and agape. *Mania* results from a mixture of eros and ludus. Manic lovers show the passion toward their loved one that is characteristic of eros, but they often idealize or even idolize their partners and they speak and think of those partners in superlatives. They alternate between feelings of ecstasy and feelings of agony. As the term "mania" suggests, a pathological element is involved: The manic lover sometimes seems to have lost his or her senses. Mania plays a role in the movies *Fatal Attraction* (in which a married man engages in a short affair with a woman who subsequently refuses to end the affair and starts blackmailing him) and *Swimfan* (in which a teenage girl obsesses over a boy who is in love with someone else).

Pragma is a mixture of storge and ludus. It is a love style rooted in logic and pragmatic thinking. Pragma develops slowly over time, just as does storge. A pragmatic lover hesitates to commit to a relationship (as with ludus) until he or she feels confident of finding the right partner. When people engage in online dating, they often show the pragmatic kind of love by developing a list of the attributes that the ideal partner should have. They then choose a potential partner according to how well the individual conforms to the list of ideal attributes.

My husband and I have two friends who are each single and looking for a partner. He suggested that we put them in touch with one another because just maybe they would like each other. But when my husband talked to our female friend, he discovered that a potential partner would need to satisfy a whole shopping list of attributes. The ideal partner would have to be a Presbyterian, live in a particular city, fall within a narrow age range, and be well-to-do. Our male friend wasn't a sufficiently close fit to these criteria. Our attempt at matchmaking turned out to be utterly unsuccessful. But our attempt well illustrates the pragmatic approach to love. The character of Charlotte in *Pride and Prejudice* provides an example of pragmatic love. Charlotte agrees to marry a man in order to gain financial security.

Agape is a mixture of eros and storge. It is an altruistic, giving kind of love. The loved one's welfare is placed before one's own welfare. The first letter to the Corinthians in the Bible (1 Corinthians 13:4–7) espouses agape as the ideal kind of love, but this kind of love is not found often today in romantic relationships. It may increase in incidence with events such as a partner's illness. But it more commonly takes the form of the love parents have for their children. Agape can be found in the movie *Untamed Heart* (in which a girl falls in love with a boy and stays with him after she finds out he has a heart defect and won't live long).

Clyde and Susan Hendrick (2006) found the theory of the colors of love as suggested by Lee intriguing, and they developed a questionnaire to measure the various styles of love in Lee's theory. Their Love Attitudes Scale (LAS) has six subscales, each of which measures one of the six styles of love. An individual then can be assigned a score for each love style so that each person has a personal profile indicating where he or she falls with regard to a particular love style. The resulting 24-item composite instrument has excellent psychometric (i.e., statistical) properties (Hendrick, Hendrick, & Dicke, 1998). The LAS has gone through several revisions. If you're interested in trying it out for yourself, Table 3.1 lists some items that are similar to those found in the LAS.

When you answer the questions in Table 3.1, score yourself on a scale from 1 to 5 ("strongly disagree" to "strongly agree") for each item. Then calculate your score for each subscale:

- Eros: items 1 to 3
- Ludus: items 4 to 6
- Storge: items 7 to 9
- Pragma: items 10 to 12
- Mania: items 13 to 15
- Agape: items 16 to 18

The higher your score on each of the subscales, the more of that particular kind of love you have for your partner.

TABLE 3.1 ITEMS TO ASSESS THE SIX DIFFERENT KINDS OF LOVE

1. My partner looks really beautiful/handsome to me.
2. There's a lot of chemistry between my partner and me.
3. My partner is my soul mate.
4. It's okay to have some secrets from my partner as long as he/she doesn't find out.
5. I've sometimes had a relationship with someone else on the side while being with my current partner.
6. It's better for my partner not to find out the details of my relationships with other people.
7. Our love is the result of a long friendship.
8. What makes our relationship so great is exactly that it developed slowly from friendship.
9. Our love is based not on some kind of magic fairy tale, but on true friendship.
10. It is important to me that my partner have a good reputation because that reputation will impact me as well.
11. Planning my career had an impact on my choice of partner.
12. Before I decided to engage in a long-term relationship with my partner, I tried to find out whether or not he/she would be a good parent.
13. I get very anxious when I feel my partner is ignoring me.
14. It's hard for me to think about anything except my partner.
15. I am always afraid that my partner may have an affair.
16. To me it's more important that my partner be happy than that I be happy.
17. I'd do anything for my partner.
18. I am glad to make sacrifices so that my partner can achieve his/her goals.

Source: Based on Hendrick et al., 1998.

The six love styles are largely independent of each other and can be linked to other traits, such as respect and intimacy. The styles seem to form attitude/belief systems that have developed over the most recent millennium of human development (Singer, 1984). Because attitudes are involved, the style profile of a person can change depending on a number of factors, such as stage of life, loved one, type of relationship, and sociodemographic features. It feels different to fall in love depending on your love style profile. Eros and mania frequently come with a great deal of emotion whereas storge, pragma, and ludus typically are not associated with strong emotion.

As mentioned above, the different love styles also correlate with some other personality traits. Levels of eros are positively correlated with agreeableness, conscientiousness, and extraversion but is negatively correlated with neuroticism. Passionate lovers also tend to have high self-esteem. Storge is generally similar to eros in how it relates to other personality traits, with the exception that it is not related to levels of agreeableness and self-esteem. Levels of ludus in turn are positively correlated with neuroticism and negatively correlated with agreeableness and conscientiousness as well as with self-disclosure. One's level of pragma is correlated positively with conscientiousness and negatively with openness to experience. Levels of mania are correlated positively with neuroticism and negatively with self-esteem. Levels of agape have been found not to be correlated with any of the aforementioned personality traits (Hendrick & Hendrick, 1986, 1987b; White, Hendrick, & Hendrick, 2004).

Not surprisingly, the love styles are also associated with specific sexual attitudes. Level of ludus is correlated positively with sexual permissiveness (casual sexuality), a finding that makes sense given that people with high levels of ludus are reluctant to commit to any one person and engage in multiple relationships over relatively short periods of time. Eros, in contrast, is associated with idealized sexuality (the concept that you are one with your partner) and monogamous sexual practices (Hendrick & Hendrick, 1987a).

There are also some gender differences connected to levels of the various kinds of love. Men are more prone to game-playing love (ludus), whereas women are more prone to friendship (storge) and practical love (pragma). When you think back to Chapter 2 and what we learned about evolutionary theories, this finding actually makes good sense. Because the investment in a potentially resulting pregnancy is smaller for men than for women, men more easily can engage in game-playing love. From an evolutionary perspective, this attitude would enable them to impregnate more women and thereby further propagate their genes. Because for women the investment in a pregnancy is much higher, it makes sense that their love style would be more influenced by practical considerations and friendship, as characterized by greater commitment to the friend or partner (Hendrick et al., 1998). There are also gender differences in what pragmatic lovers search for in a partner. As the definition of the love style would lead you to expect, pragmatic lovers tend to seek specific characteristics in a partner. But female pragmatic lovers also often look for a partner who is romantic and passionate (Hammock & Richardson, 2011).

High levels of eros and storge are generally related to higher satisfaction in relationships, whereas the game playing of ludus is related to lower satisfaction (Grote & Frieze, 1994). Couples in successful relationships also are more likely to be in erotic rather than ludic relationships.

One research study related television viewing behavior to the different love styles (Hetsroni, 2012). The study showed that the long-term habit of viewing a particular kind of program may correspond to the viewer's preference for particular love styles. For example, levels of ludus correlated positively with the watching of TV news. Levels of pragma also correlated positively with watching news, and they correlated negatively with the watching of television series that included love themes, like soap operas. Levels of eros correlated positively with watching soap operas and other series centered on love themes. Levels of agape, mania, and storge did not have any significant correlations with TV viewing.

Interestingly, young people and their parents do not seem to be similar in their love styles (Inman-Amos, Hendrick, & Hendrick, 1994). Also, no differences in love profiles between heterosexual and homosexual males have been found (Adler, Hendrick, & Hendrick, 1986).

CHAPTER 3

STERNBERG'S DUPLEX THEORY OF LOVE

Robert Sternberg's duplex theory of love consists of two different parts—one that suggests a taxonomy of love styles on the basis of three components (intimacy, passion, and commitment) and one that conceptualizes love as a story (Sternberg, 2006).

Let us begin with the triangular subtheory of love. Sternberg suggests that we can view love as a triangle whose sides are formed by three different components: intimacy, passion, and commitment. Depending on how much of each of these components is present in a relationship, the sides of the love triangle vary in size. *Intimacy* is associated with feelings of closeness and connectedness. High levels of intimacy imply that you feel you can rely on your partner in times of need, and have a high regard for and a mutual understanding with your partner (Sternberg & Grajek, 1984). *Passion* is related to physical attraction and sexual feelings. However, although sexual feelings often dominate passion, they do not have to. Passion involves feelings of excitement, strong attraction, and sometimes infatuation. A need for affiliation, nurturance, and escape, for example, can also contribute to passion. *Commitment* is the decision first to love one's partner and second to maintain that love over time. These two parts of commitment do not always occur together. People can decide they love others but not commit to their loved ones over the long term. Moreover, people may be committed to the maintenance of relationships without ever having admitted to themselves that they love the significant other. The three components of love interact. If you're feeling very intimate with another person, this feeling may lead to greater passion or greater commitment; if you are feeling committed to a relationship, this feeling may lead to your experiencing greater intimacy.

When you look at the three components of love in combination, eight possible kinds of love result. Keep in mind, however, that in real life, aspects of relationships are hardly ever as cleanly separable into components as they are in theory. A relationship may resemble one kind of love more closely than it does another, but it is unlikely to represent a pure case of any of the love types.

Table 3.2 shows the combinations of the three components and the types of love that result.

To summarize the table, if neither intimacy, passion, nor commitment is present, the result is nonlove. If there is only intimacy, the result is liking and friendship. The presence of only passion leads to infatuated love; and empty love has neither intimacy nor passion, only the commitment to maintain the relationship. A relationship that is characterized by both intimacy and passion is romantic love. Companionate love possesses the intimacy component but also a commitment to the relationship over the long term. Fatuous love does not involve any intimacy, only passion and commitment. And finally, consummate (complete) love involves all of the components: intimacy, passion, and commitment.

Because many if not most relationships involve all three components in various degrees, we can depict them in the shape of a triangle, where each side of the triangle corresponds to the

TABLE 3.2 **TAXONOMY OF KINDS OF LOVE**

	Intimacy	Passion	Commitment
Nonlove	No	No	No
Friendship	Yes	No	No
Infatuated love	No	Yes	No
Empty love	No	No	Yes
Romantic love	Yes	Yes	No
Companionate love	Yes	No	Yes
Fatuous love	No	Yes	Yes
Consummate love	Yes	Yes	Yes

amount of one component. For example, when all three components are present equally, the result is an equilateral triangle. Furthermore, the area of the love triangle can depict the amount of love: The greater the amount of love, the greater the area of the triangle.

There are actually quite a number of love triangles that people can have: (a) real and ideal triangles, (b) self- and other-perceived triangles, and (c) triangles of feelings and of actions. A real triangle represents the love you have for a particular person, and an ideal triangle represents the ideal configuration of components of love you would like to have. A self-perceived triangle reflects how you feel about the relationship and which components you feel are present and in what amounts. But our own perceptions and those of our partners do not always correspond. Therefore, there is also a triangle reflecting the perceptions of the partner as to which components are present and in what amounts.

Finally, the theory suggests that people's feelings are not always in accord with their actions. Therefore, we distinguish between triangles of feelings and triangles of actions. Take John, for example. He feels that there is a great deal of intimacy in his relationship with his girlfriend of 8 months, Tanya. So his feelings triangle indicates a substantial amount of intimacy. Intimacy manifests itself in actions such as sharing one's thoughts and desires with another person and spending time together. But John never really shares his views, hopes, and desires with his girlfriend. His action triangle therefore differs significantly from his feelings triangle because he does not act on the intimacy he feels in his relationship with Tanya. Unfortunately for John, Tanya is dissatisfied with the relationship because John seems to be unable to express his feelings.

Intimacy and commitment are related to attachment security (see Chapter 2): The more securely a person is attached, the more intimacy and commitment he or she is likely to feel in a relationship. If you think about it, it follows that you can open up more and be more intimate with a person if you feel secure in your relationship. Security also makes it easier to commit to the relationship because it eases concerns about being betrayed or abandoned. Levels of intimacy and commitment, in turn, predict greater relationship satisfaction (Madey & Rodgers, 2009).

The second subtheory in the duplex theory involves love as a story. Sternberg suggests that all love triangles emanate from stories. From the time we are children, we observe in daily life different love relationships and form conceptions of what love can potentially be. Our personal attributes interact with our environment, and we create our own stories about what we believe love to be. We then try to realize these stories in our lives. Different people fit in our love stories to varying degrees. In general, a relationship is more likely to succeed when a partner's story is compatible with one's own.

The number of possible love stories probably approaches infinity. Nevertheless, some stories have greater prevalence than others and appear again and again in Sternberg's research analyzing accounts of love in movies, literature, and people's descriptions of their relationships (Sternberg, 1998). Sternberg's most recent list (2006) includes 26 kinds of stories. Table 3.3 presents a selection of the love stories.

Some of the love stories are more common than others. For example, you will find more people who have *gardening* as a love story than have *horror* as a love story. Depending on one's story, a person has a characteristic way of behaving. A person with a *history* love story will collect mementos and will likely be able to recount in detail and with dates lots of events in the couple's history. A person with a *science* love story, in contrast, will typically dissect interactions in the relationship and analyze details to understand more about the character of the relationship.

TABLE 3.3 **SELECTION OF LOVE STORIES**

Addiction	Strong, anxious attachment
	Clinging behavior; anxiety at thought of losing partner
Business	Relationships as business propositions; money is power; partners in close relationships as business partners
Cookbook	Doing things in a certain way (recipe) in a relationship makes the relationship more likely to work out; departure from recipe for success leads to an increased likelihood of failure
Fantasy	Expectation of being saved by a knight in shining armor or of marrying a princess and living happily ever after
Game	Love as a game or sport
Gardening	Relationships need to be continually nurtured and tended to
Government	
Autocratic	One partner dominates or controls the other
Democratic	Two partners share power equally
History	Events of relationship form an indelible record; a lot of recordkeeping, either mental or material
Horror	Relationship becomes interesting when you terrorize or are terrorized by your partner
Police	You've got to keep close tabs on your partner to make sure he or she toes the line, or you need to be under surveillance to make sure you behave
Sacrifice	To love is to give of oneself or for someone to give of himself or herself to you
Science	Love can be understood, analyzed, and dissected, just like any other natural phenomenon
Travel	Love is a journey

Source: Sternberg (2006, p. 192).

There is significant overlap between Sternberg's love stories and other theories on love. The story of love as a game, for example, is similar to Lee's (1977) ludus, and the story of love as a fantasy resembles conceptions of romantic love (Sternberg, 1986; Walster & Walster, 1981).

Having a certain love story can restrict one's horizon when a person believes love or a loving relationship must take one form or another. If another person does not fit the story, then he or she may be seen as inadequate. As you may have noticed, some of the love stories involve complementary roles. The police story, for example, has one person who keeps track and one person who is being kept track of. You look for a partner who shares your story or at least has a story that is compatible with yours, but obviously you are not always looking for someone who resembles you.

Each story has potential advantages and disadvantages, and what works well depends on the person's cultural milieu. Generally, some stories have more potential for success than others: The story of love as a game may lead someone to look for a new partner soon after the newness and excitement of the relationship wears off, whereas the conception of love as gardening will likely result in a partner's trying to tend to and nurture the relationship on a long-term basis.

Our love stories represent both causes and effects. Having a particular story makes us more likely to behave in a certain way, and by means of our behavior we shape our environment and elicit reactions from our partners and others. As we grow older, our experiences and interactions with others may further shape our love stories.

Questionnaires are available to assess both the three components of love—intimacy, passion, and commitment—and people's love stories. In two validation studies (Sternberg, Hojjat, & Barnes, 2001), participants completed both the triangular scales and the love story questionnaire. Travel, gardening, democratic government, and history were the most popular stories; horror, autocratic government, and game stories were among the least popular. There were some gender differences, with women favoring the travel story and men favoring stories such as art, sacrifice, and science fiction.

The two subtheories differed in their prediction of satisfaction. All three components of the triangular theory positively predicted relationship satisfaction. In contrast, none of the stories positively predicted satisfaction; however, a number of stories were negatively correlated with satisfaction, among them business, game, horror, and science fiction. The results of the study also confirmed that having similar love stories and similar triangular love profiles increases people's satisfaction in their relationships.

CLARK: COMMUNAL RESPONSIVENESS AS LOVE

Margaret Clark conceptualizes love in quite a different way compared with most of the other researchers we've looked at in this chapter (Clark, 2006; Clark & Mills, 2012). She suggests that love exists when people show consistent communal responsiveness toward each other. But before we proceed, what is communal responsiveness? A person exhibits communal responsiveness when he or she watches out for another's well-being and needs and desires. The person also tries to help and support the other. This concept is probably easiest to understand with the help of some examples.

Imagine a husband and a wife. The husband starts talking about a vacation they took a long time ago. He starts wondering about the name of a restaurant they visited during that time. He can't remember and asks his wife, who remembers a name but believes it's not the name for which they're looking. They start joking and making bets about the name of the restaurant and recall the happy times they had during their vacation. They feel very intimately connected during their interaction.

As another example, imagine a small child who has been stung in the foot by a bee and develops an itchy, swollen foot. She suffers greatly all day. Her mother tells her that she understands how it hurts and recounts a story of when she herself was stung by a wasp. She applies ice to the child's foot and, from time to time, sprays anti-itch lotion on the sting. She also cooks her daughter's favorite dinner that night as a reward for her being so valiant. The mother empathizes with her daughter and shows through her actions how much she cares about her well-being. She comforts her child and, through her actions, strengthens the child's resilience.

In both examples, one person cares deeply about another and exhibits signs of empathy, connectedness, and intimacy. This experience occurs without the giver expecting anything in return. The focus is squarely on the other, although there is an implicit trust that the other person will take care of the giver if the giver ever needs help. This feeling of giving without the expectation of anything particular in return is what characterizes communal relationships. A communal relationship is two-sided, however, in the reciprocal desire to value the needs of the other without expecting a tit for tat. In this respect, they can be contrasted with exchange relationships, in which there is such an expectation.

In this view, a successful communal relationship is one that involves being sensitive to the partner's needs, helping and supporting without expecting immediate payback, being so comfortable that one can disclose one's needs and goals, and being confident that one will actually be supported in times of need. A relationship of this kind can lead to personal growth as well as increased physical and mental health (Clark & Finkel, 2005). In fact, Clark believes that assessing relationship quality in terms of communal responsiveness works better than counting the number of conflicts in a relationship or even assessing a person's satisfaction within the relationship (Clark & Monin, 2006).

Communal responsiveness can take different forms. One is helping out when a person is in need of assistance. Another one is supporting a person when he or she is trying to achieve a goal. This goal could be something as simple as a husband's supporting the need of his wife to take a break from their young children and meet with her friends from time to time in the evening, or as ambitious as a man supporting a spouse so that she can complete a degree while he works full-time at his job. A communal relationship also can be expressed by a collaboration with a partner to do something that is beneficial for one or both persons, such as renovating a house together or planning a weekend getaway. Another expression of a communal relationship is the exhibition of caring behavior when the partner makes a mistake of some sort. For example, if a husband forgets to do the shopping he promised to do after work, and the wife shows understanding and compassion, acknowledging what a hard and busy day he had, the wife is displaying communal responsiveness. Communal responsiveness even can be symbolic, as when one sends a greeting card to a person who is hospitalized or when one delivers a meal to a family with a new baby.

In all cases of responsiveness, the focus is on the recipient and not on the giver. The actions provide the recipient with comfort and support. The communal responsiveness signifies to the recipient that the partner deeply cares about him or her, which in turn makes it easier for both partners to open up and reveal vulnerabilities, needs, and desires.

An important feature of communal responsiveness is that it is noncontingent; that is, one partner will help without expecting reciprocity. But noncontingency is just as important on the side of the recipient. Acceptance of an offer of help is therefore a significant part of communal responsiveness, as is thanking the giver.

Communal responsiveness is shown in many different situations. People essentially maintain an implicit hierarchy. The higher up one is in the hierarchy, the more responsiveness that person will be shown. Highest in the hierarchy are usually one's spouse and children, and further down you find friends. Somewhat lower may be neighbors with whom one is not particularly close. The hierarchy has the shape of a triangle, with very few relationships at the top and progressively more as you move down in the hierarchy (Reis, Clark, & Holmes, 2004). Obviously, being one of the few people at the top of someone's hierarchy represents a relationship that is different from being near the bottom, a position you would likely share with many others.

There are also implicit hierarchies with respect to how much responsiveness people expect from others. One typically expects people high in the hierarchy, such as one's spouse, to take on more communal responsibility for them than they would expect of people lower in the hierarchy. Also, the more responsiveness you expect from another person, the likelier you are to open up to that person about your needs.

Often, the hierarchies of two individuals in a relationship are symmetrical, but they do not have to be. In the relationship with their children, for example, parents typically feel a much greater responsibility for the well-being of their small children than the children feel for the well-being of the parents. Even though hierarchies can be asymmetrical, however, the amounts of love the people in the relationship feel do not need to be unequal.

Clark and Monin (2006) have suggested that we can speak of love when communal responsiveness surpasses an implicit threshold of communal strength. Other factors may play a role as well, such as how long two people have been in a relationship characterized by high communal strength and how long they expect to remain in that relationship. If a partner cannot feel certain that his or her loved one will exhibit the degree of communal responsiveness that he or she expects, sooner or later that partner may begin to wonder whether the relationship in question truly is a love relationship.

Often in life, expectations and reality do not correspond. The amount of responsiveness a person should ideally show and the amount he or she does show often differ. In assessing the degree to which people feel loved, actual responsiveness seems to be more important than the ideal level of responsiveness.

CHAPTER 3

EXCURSION: FRIENDSHIP

Friendships are an important part of many people's lives. We start forming friendships as young children, and most of us would like to have friends until the very end of life. All the theories of love we discuss in this chapter treat friendship as one type of love. Sternberg's triangular theory of love (1986), for example, suggests that when people feel very intimate with each other, they are friends. Other studies have also shown that intimacy is the component that differentiates friendships from other, more formal relationships we have with others (Schneider, 2000).

Friends also display communal responsiveness toward each other as conceptualized by Clark and Monin (2006). They care about each other and support each other when they go through difficult times or try to achieve ambitious goals. Lee (1973) and Clyde and Susan Hendrick (2006) refer to a type of love based on friendship as well: storge. This kind of love develops relatively slowly and commitment plays a big part in it. It is for this reason that friendships often last a long time, even a lifetime, whereas romantic relationships tend to break up more easily. Finally, Ellen Berscheid (2010) includes friendship in her category of companionate love.

But will a person befriend just about anyone? How do we go about choosing our friends? Typically, people develop friendships with the ones they're in touch with often and who are similar to themselves (Amichai-Hamburger, Kingsbury, & Schneider, 2013; Clark & Drewry, 1985). That means, for example, that you're more likely to develop a friendship with someone who lives in your area than with someone who lives in another part of the country. A study by Mazur and Richards (2011) has shown that even when online on social networking sites, people mostly interact with others who are geographically close to them. And just as with romantic relationships, we make friends mostly with those who share some of our characteristics, such as race, or interests (Schneider, 2000). We will discuss the importance of similarity in romantic relationships in more detail in Chapters 6, 8, and 9, which cover attraction, online dating, and the role of personality traits in love.

The Internet is a great tool for finding people who share our interests or other characteristics that are important to us. So it probably doesn't come as a surprise that there are many online groups in which people discuss common interests. There are groups for almost anything you can imagine, from collecting ancient coins to treating rare diseases, and even groups in which people resell baby clothes for boy–girl–girl sets of triplets.

An important element of friendship is that friends actually get to share good times together (Fehr, 1995). Nevertheless, as indicated in Clark's concept of communal love, friends do provide critical support to each other during challenging times. Thus, friendships are in many ways important to people's well-being.

BERSCHEID'S FOUR KINDS OF LOVE

Ellen Berscheid has suggested that there are four different kinds of love (Berscheid, 2006a, 2006b, 2010). From her perspective, one kind of love should be differentiated from another when (a) each is associated with different behaviors and (b) each has different underlying causes. With respect to the causes for a certain kind of behavior or love, Berscheid distinguishes historical and immediate causes. Historical causes are the ones that reach back far into the history of human evolution and address the question of why a certain kind of love developed. Immediate causes are the situations or events that trigger a certain behavior.

In her view, the four different kinds of love that satisfy these criteria, and that are also representative of the basic types of love, are attachment love, compassionate love, companionate love, and romantic love. A given relationship may be represented by one kind of love at one time and by another kind of love at a different time.

Attachment love involves attachment, as we have already discussed in Chapter 2. Behaviors that are characteristic of attachment love are the ones that promote proximity to another person who is typically older, stronger, and more experienced. By seeking proximity, an individual is looking for comfort and security. In the case of attachment love, the historical cause lies in the importance for human infants of staying close to their caregivers to increase their chances for survival. The immediate cause for behavior associated with attachment love is a situation in which a person feels threatened.

Compassionate love is the kind of love in which one looks out for the well-being of others. One acts to promote the well-being of another even if it is not advantageous (or even if it is disadvantageous) to the individual performing the act. Compassionate love has also been called "altruistic love" or "charitable love," and is similar to Lee's agape and Clark's communal love. Characteristic behaviors associated with compassionate love are actions aimed at alleviating the distress of another person. The historical cause of compassionate love is the fact that since ancient times humans have lived mostly in groups and are often dependent on one another for survival. The immediate cause is the perception that someone else is in distress and needs help.

Companionate love, in contrast to attachment and compassionate love, is based to a large extent on principles of reward and punishment. We affiliate with the people who we think like us and who make us feel good. We try to stay away from the ones who make us feel bad. Companionate love is similar to Lee's storge and to pragmatic love, and to Sternberg's companionate love and friendship. Characteristic behaviors are that we try to maintain friendship and closeness with the people we like, often by means of actions that we believe the other person will appreciate. The historical cause lies again in our need of others for survival. We tend to associate and cluster with others to increase our chances of survival. Immediate causes for companionate love are perceived similarity and physical attractiveness (Berscheid & Regan, 2005), among others—in short, any features that make you like another. Companionate love often is enduring over a long period of time. A recent longitudinal study, however, found that within the first year of marriage, both romantic love and companionate love typically decline (Hatfield, Pillemer, O'Brien, & Le, 2008).

Romantic love is similar to Sternberg's romantic love and Lee's eros. Sexual desire is often associated with romantic love. Berscheid and others (Meyers & Berscheid, 1997; Regan, 1998) have suggested that the difference between romantic love and companionate love is the presence of sexual desire. Characteristic behaviors are flirting and trying to get the attention of a desired mate as well as kissing and other affiliative acts and behaviors directed toward mate retention. The historical cause of romantic love lies in our evolutionary striving to reproduce and pass on our genes to another generation. Immediate causes are still not well understood, but again include perceived similarity, geographic proximity, and physical attraction.

As you have seen in this chapter, there have been a number of efforts to categorize love and distinguish different kinds of love. Some kinds, like romantic love, can be found in almost all approaches. Others overlap to a certain extent between theories or can be found in only one theory.

In sum, there are multiple approaches to understanding love in all its different forms. The approaches overlap somewhat, and at this point there is no clear evidence that any one of these approaches is distinctively right and the others wrong. Rather, the different approaches are largely complementary and in combination can help us understand the wonder and joy of the experience of love.

Cultural Theories of Love

hat is the role of culture in love? Is love universal? Does it take different forms in different cultures? These are some of the questions we address in this chapter.

IS ROMANTIC LOVE UNIVERSAL?

Although romantic love may seem like a very natural thing to you, many scholars have viewed it as a Western invention that is not found in other cultures. This view has not been unique to psychologists. It also has been widespread among other professionals, such as anthropologists. Historians have subscribed to the same notion (see Aries, 1962): Stone (1989) has suggested that romantic love does not exist in non-Western countries, except possibly for the elite of those countries who have the time to cultivate romantic love (see also Lindholm, 1998a, 1998b).

Evolutionary psychologists, in contrast, argue that passionate love is innate to human nature and is based on biological processes that are universal, applying to people of all cultures.

A landmark study by Jankowiak and Fischer (1992), which became the basis for many subsequent studies, set out to investigate if it is true that people in many if not all cultures of the world experience romantic love. They used data from a standard cross-cultural sample (SCCS; Murdock & White, 1969). First, they examined the data and also analyzed available information about folklore and other ethnographies. Overall, the researchers found a sufficient amount of useful information for 166 societies. For each society the information was screened for signs that love exists in that country, and the researchers actually made a distinction between love and lust, which is unusual in studies of this kind. The researchers looked for certain signs that would serve as indicators that love was present during the first 2 years of a couple's involvement. The indicators they used were (a) whether people described suffering and a desire for their beloved when the partner was not present, (b) the presence of love songs and traditions that emphasize the motivation behind intimate love relationships, (c) reports of passionate love in a given culture, (d) accounts of people leaving their homes or communities due to their love for someone else, and (e) reports by ethnographers about romantic love in a culture.

Using these indicators, the researchers found that romantic love was present in 147 out of the 166 cultures (88.5%). For the remaining 19 cultures, they were not able to find signs indicating that people experienced romantic love. This, however, does not necessarily mean that romantic love does not exist in those cultures; it simply was not mentioned as such in the information available.

Although the results show that romantic love is nearly universal in the world, we cannot draw the conclusion that every person will fall in love. Jankowiak and Fischer (1992) have suggested that although romantic love can be controlled by some cultural variables, it can never be entirely suppressed. It isn't clear whether people fall in love less often when their society disapproves of romantic love. However, it is possible that people fall in love more or less often depending on their culture's social organization and ideology. We'll find out more about this later in the chapter.

WHY DO WE FALL IN LOVE WITH SOMEONE?

The beginning, and sometimes the end, of the experience of romantic love is falling in love. Falling in love can be quick or slow, intense or subtle. It can be triggered by many factors. Research has found that some of the antecedents of falling in love are (Aron, Dutton, Aron, & Iverson, 1989; Pines, 2005):

- *Reciprocal liking:* How much do two people like each other?
- *Appearance:* How much is someone attracted by another's bodily features?
- *Personality traits:* How much is someone attracted to another person's personality traits, such as intelligence, empathy, and humor?
- *Similarity:* How much do two people have in common; for example, sociocultural background, experiences, interests, or attitudes?

- *Familiarity:* How much time do two people spend together?
- *Social influence:* Do family and friends (as well as other people or social networks that matter) approve or disapprove of the potential partner?
- *Filling needs:* Does one person fill the other's needs and show that he or she cares? For example, does the partner make the individual happy, ease feelings of loneliness, or give presents as a token of appreciation?
- *Arousal:* Does the person experience strong physiological reactions when he or she meets the potential mate? Does the individual experience an accelerated heartbeat or more rapid breathing?
- *Readiness:* Is the individual ready for a new relationship, or is he or she still struggling with the loss of a previous relationship?
- *Isolation:* Do two people get to spend time alone together, or are they largely isolated from each other?
- *Other cues:* Are there other things about a person that make one attracted to him or her—for example, his or her accent or color of hair?

As you can see, quite a number of different variables can influence whether two people fall in love. But which ones matter to most people, and are there any differences between people belonging to different cultures? Aron and his colleagues (1989) found that people most often mentioned reciprocal liking, personality, and appearance as factors that influenced their falling in love with each other. A study by Pines (2001) also found that personality and appearance matter significantly when people fall in love. Researchers also found some gender differences in that men place more of an emphasis on appearance than women, and women put a higher priority on personality and arousal. They did not find gender differences in a number of other variables, such as similarity, familiarity, filling needs, and reciprocal liking. A similar picture emerged in a cross-cultural study by Sprecher and her colleagues (1994), in which reciprocal liking and personality emerged as the most important factors. Interestingly, Sprecher did not find any significant cultural differences between the United States and Japan except for the variable of social standing, which was significantly more important to Japanese participants than to American participants.

A recent study by Riela, Rodriguez, Aron, Xu, and Acevedo (2010) employed both narrative methods and self-ratings to shed more light on possible differences between diverse cultures. Participants wrote accounts of their most recent experience of falling in love. They also rated themselves on how quickly they had fallen in love, and they were given a list of antecedents and asked which of those had played a role in their falling in love. A total of 50 men and 111 women participated in the American part of the study; 29 men and 49 women participated in China. The mean age of participants in both countries was 21 years, and all participants reported they had fallen in love at least once in their lives (with the average number of times they had fallen in love being 1.72, $SD = 0.92$). Chinese participants reported more recent love experiences than White Americans ($M = 2.79$ for Chinese participants and $M = 1.49$ for White Americans, $p = .032$). Asian Americans' average number of love experiences ($M = 2.06$) fell between those two groups and did not differ significantly from the average of either other group. There were no cultural or ethnic differences for the number of times participants had been in love. Americans mentioned familiarity significantly more often than did Chinese participants (Americans 68%, Chinese 18%), whereas Chinese mentioned personality (Americans 22%, Chinese 55%), filling needs (Americans 42%, Chinese 72%), and arousal (Americans 23%, Chinese 78%) significantly more often. It is interesting that the cultural differences the study found were in many cases due not to differences between the American sample as a whole and the Chinese sample, but to differences between the Asian American part of the sample and the Chinese sample.

CHAPTER 4

WHAT DOES IT MEAN TO BE IN LOVE WITH SOMEONE?

Even if romantic love occurs in many or even all cultures of the world, it is still reasonable to assume that the experience of being in love is colored by one's cultural values and the society to which one belongs. In trying to ascertain what differences, if any, exist between features of love that are universal and features that are culture specific, it is helpful to assume, although with less-than-absolute certainty, that universal features primarily relate to mate selection, retention, and reproduction, whereas culturally influenced features are ones that pertain to cultural rituals of love and mating.

In order to understand some of these cultural rituals, deMunck, Korotayev, deMunck, and Khaltourina (2011) undertook a study including the United States, Lithuania, and Russia. One part of the study used an etic strategy, and another part used an emic strategy. An etic approach is one that studies a culture from the outside, using categories imposed by the culture doing the studying. An emic approach studies a culture from the inside, using categories that people from the studied culture generate. Etic approaches adopt a more universalistic stance, emic studies a more particularistic stance. The first (etic) part of the study had participants rate various statements about love to indicate how much they agreed or disagreed with each of the statements. There were 14 statements, including "Love is blind" and "Sexual attraction is not necessary for love." A total of 624 Americans, 296 Russians, and 237 Lithuanians participated in the study. People from all three cultures agreed on 5 statements as constituting the "core" of romantic love:

1. Physical attraction is a critical component of love.
2. One would do anything for one's beloved.

3. Lovers incessantly think about their beloved.
4. Love is what makes a person happiest in life.
5. Being loved makes someone a more resilient and better person.

The first statement relates to the eros component of love, whereas the second statement captures the essence of altruistic love (agape). The third statement reflects the tendency of lovers to engage in intrusive thinking about the beloved (also sometimes called limerence). The fourth statement relates to a concept that Lindholm (1995, 1998a) calls transcendence: the feeling that the union of two lovers results in something more meaningful than just the two lovers—essentially, that the whole is greater than the sum of its parts. The fifth statement reflects aspects of both transcendence and altruism.

When you look at those five core statements, you will notice that they do not really describe concrete attributes of love. Rather, they center on the causes and effects of love. DeMunck and his colleagues (2011) suggested that their results point toward a dynamic model of love that comprises two main processes. The first process is one of arousal that captures the attention of the lover and prompts the couple to get together. The second process is a feeling of increased well-being as a result of the partnership, which in turn increases the prospects of a continuing love relationship.

The second part of the study employed an emic approach, in which participants were asked freely to list characteristics that they associate with romantic love. There were 80 participants from each country. As expected, most of the core features of love identified in the first part of the study also were mentioned in the free lists that the participants created. The only feature that did not appear in the lists of all three countries was intrusive thinking. People in all countries agreed that being in love meant being together. But joy, for example, was associated with love in the United States more than in Russia or Lithuania. A feature that Russians and Lithuanians associated with love and that was not mentioned by Americans was taking a walk.

After having a look at the lists that participants in each country produced, the researchers collapsed the features into categories to get a better overview of the data. These categories and their rankings reflect differences between the countries and also indicate that, in their view of love, Lithuanians and Russians resemble each other much more than either group resembles Americans. The emic approach gives us quite a different picture of what people consider love to be from that obtained with the etic approach. When the researchers let participants actively determine what features of love they felt to be important, cultural differences did emerge. There was agreement across all countries that love is a strong feeling and that lovers ultimately want to be together. But the importance of nature in love was most pronounced in Russia, was less so in Lithuania, and was almost completely ignored in the United States. Altruism, on the other hand, was more important in the United States than in Lithuania and Russia.

The authors also conducted focus groups in each country. They found that Russians and Lithuanians see love as unreal and liken it to a fairy tale, expecting it at some point either to come to an end or to give way to a more real and enduring kind of relationship that lacks the initial excitement of romantic love. Only then, they feel, do "real" love and friendship set in.

In the United States, participants did not perceive romantic love as unreal or as an illusion. Because Americans (in contrast with Lithuanians and Russians) also include friendship in romantic love, it is plausible that Lithuanians and Russians fall in love much more quickly than Americans. And that is just what the study found: Ninety percent of Lithuanians reported that they fell in love within a month or less, whereas 58% of Americans fell in love within a time frame of 2 months to a year.

INDIVIDUALISM, COLLECTIVISM, AND LOVE

In psychology, one way to differentiate cultural groups of the world is to look at the relationship between a person and his or her social in-group—in particular, the family. If you are very involved with your family and feel you must consider their needs and feelings when you are in love with someone, love and its dynamics might play out quite differently than if you do not consider your social in-group's feelings about your relationship. There are different definitions of individualism, but for our purposes, we'll examine what has been called self-contained individualism (Sampson, 1977). This is the desire of a person to be as self-sufficient as possible and the tendency to perceive any dependence, both of the person on other people and of other people on that person, with ambivalence. As you can imagine, a person's drive to be as independent as possible can conflict with the need for a partner, so it may be assumed that self-contained individualism affects love for a partner in a negative way. This is curious because in cultures that are characterized as individualistic, love-based marriage is seen as an ideal, and yet the individualism can interfere with the development and maintenance of a loving relationship.

Karen and Kenneth Dion have conducted numerous studies to find out more about the relationship to love of individualism and collectivism. They found that people who are more individualistic exhibit a lower likelihood of ever having been in love (K. K. Dion & Dion, 1991). Such people were also more likely to endorse a ludic love style, which, as you may remember from Chapter 3, involves a game-playing perspective on love. When participants had been in love before, greater individualism was associated with a perception of their relationships as less rewarding and less deep. Generally, the more individualistic a person was found to be, the lower the quality of the person's love for his or her partner. By analyzing data from the General Social Survey (GSS) for the year 1993, K. L. Dion and Dion (2005) found that people who are high in individualism tend to report less happiness in their marriages as well as lower satisfaction with their family life and friends. Not only does individualism affect romantic love relationships, but it also influences the relationship of members within a family. In families that place more value on individualism, ties between the family members are usually looser and mutual help is not taken for granted or expected. Additionally, when adult offspring had to support their parents, they often "outsourced" the help and hired others to perform the physical care that was needed. In fact, it seems that adult offspring often felt it was more a matter of duty than one of affection to take care of their elderly parents. Their parents in turn valued their own independence and did not want or expect their children to assist with their lives as they got older. Parents were afraid it might put a strain on the relationship with their children if they suddenly became dependent on their children's help. They wanted their children to like them, and they were not sure if their children would like them as much if put in the position of being obliged to take care of them (Pyke & Bengtson, 1996). As long as older adults are in good physical and mental condition, their individualism and related attitudes may work for them. Once they get in a situation where they are dependent on help, however, individualism will not serve them quite so well. The parents may feel resentful that they have to accept assistance and the children may not be as willing to provide the care that is now required. In some cases, older parents have even chosen to reduce contact with their children so as not to have to acknowledge their growing dependency on assistance, which in turn results in less companionship and assistance as they grow older (Pyke, 1999).

Let us now turn to collectivism. Whereas individualism is found mostly in Western cultures, collectivism is more likely to be found in Eastern cultures. In collectivistic cultures, people are embedded in a whole network of relationships with their family and close friends, and experience the resulting dependencies in their lives. People's decisions, therefore, do not depend only on what they think is best for themselves; people also consciously take into account what effect a decision (and, in the case of love, a romantic relationship) is likely to have on their social network. Collectivism is related to the view of love as pragmatic, based on friendship, and having altruistic goals (Dion & Dion, 2005). Women in collectivistic cultures tend to endorse an agapic view of love more commonly than women in individualistic cultures and consequently place greater emphasis on having a network of close relationships (K. K. Dion & Dion, 1993; K. L. Dion & Dion, 1993).

Ingersoll-Dayton, Campbell, Kurokawa, and Saito (1996) compared how marriages develop over the long term in the United States versus Japan. The researchers found that, in the United States, marriages start out with a relatively high level of intimacy. The goal of the respective partners is to keep the intimacy of the relationship while maintaining a separate identity. Japanese marriages, on the other hand, are at first characterized by the many obligations the married couple have to the other people in their social network. Intimacy develops later in life as a result of both the death of close family members to whom the couple had obligations and the husband's greater willingness to share affection with the wife.

Cultures placing greater emphasis on collectivism generally find family bonds and the associated interdependence and mutual assistance very important. They view their family members in a more positive light than do people who are more individualistically oriented. It is easy to see how care of elderly parents in collectivistic cultures is marked more by affection than by duty. Adults' level of commitment to their parents is often very high (Pyke & Bengtson, 1996).

Why is it that individualism and collectivism have such a profound impact on the way people experience and construct their lives? It is largely a matter of how a person understands himself or herself. Generally, Western psychology has adopted the view that each person is a separate entity. Asian psychology, in contrast, views the individual as part of a complex network of relationships. When you perceive yourself as an individual with clear boundaries and as separate from all other people, loving someone is your chance to break through those boundaries and escape the quintessential loneliness that being a separate individual entails. Love becomes the bridge that connects you to others. This connection, however, is voluntary. If a relationship does not give you what you expect, it is your choice whether to leave the relationship. In the Asian perspective, there is more emphasis on acknowledging and strengthening the bonds that already exist. Because each person is seen as part of a network of bonds, it is not considered necessary for persons to verbally confirm those bonds by asking if another loves them or by announcing their love to someone else. Their love is expressed more by what they do than by what they say (Dion & Dion, 2006). Thus, how people conceptualize themselves can have a significant impact on how they love and what they expect of love.

THE IMPACT OF CULTURE ON OUR EXPERIENCE OF LOVE

Culture can influence not only whether and how quickly we fall in love, but also how we experience love. Within the United States, Chinese Americans experience higher levels of passionate love than do European Americans; Pacific Islanders are more likely to experience companionate love (Doherty, Hatfield, Thompson, & Choo, 1994). Virtually nothing is straightforward in psychology, however, as it also has been found that European Americans sometimes experience more intense passionate love than do Chinese Americans (Gao, 2001). When people of different nationalities were asked whether they were currently in love, Russians were the people who were found to be most in love (67%), Americans were in the middle (58%), and the Japanese were the least likely to be in love (52%; Sprecher et al., 1994). There are also cultural differences influencing whether someone of a given culture will consent to marry another who is all they want in a partner but whom they do not love. In Pakistan and India, about half of all respondents said they could imagine marrying a person they do not love, whereas the percentage of people agreeing to such a union was very low in Japan (2%) and the United States (4%; Levine, Sato, Hashimoto, & Verma, 1995).

In their research on love, David Schmitt and David Buss (2000) created a dimension of love they call emotional investment. Emotional investment comprises a variety of the core features of love that we have discussed in previous chapters, and is measured by self-ratings on a list of adjectives such as *loving, affectionate, cuddlesome, compassionate,* and *passionate*. In line with the evolutionary model of Belsky, Steinberg, and Draper (1991), known as the BSD model, the expectation is that children who grow up in a highly stressful environment (e.g., with inconsistent or insensitive parenting, in harsh physical environments, or with few economic resources) will exhibit lower levels of emotional investment than children who grow up in environments with less stress. In fact, such a lower level of emotional investment is also associated with earlier puberty, a higher number of offspring, and short-term mating strategies (Chisholm, 1999; Kirkpatrick, 1998; Schmitt, 2005).

To investigate the impact of culture on love in more detail, Schmitt teamed up with several colleagues and embarked on the International Sexuality Description Project (ISDP; see Schmitt, 2006; Schmitt et al., 2003, 2004). They had 15,234 participants from 48 nations complete several psychological scales and additionally used data from other sources about the respective cultures. The countries with the lowest levels of emotional commitment were Tanzania ($M = 5.44$), Hong Kong ($M = 5.54$), and Japan ($M = 5.60$), whereas the countries with the highest levels of emotional investment were the United States ($M = 7.53$), Slovenia ($M = 7.47$), and Cyprus ($M = 7.38$). Nationality had a significant effect on emotional investment (Schmitt et al., 2009). When the researchers aggregated different countries into regions of the world, they also found that region had a significant effect on emotional investment. North America exhibited levels of emotional investment that were significantly higher than those in all other regions of the world, and East Asia had levels of emotional investment that were significantly lower than those of all other world regions.

Next the researchers examined how stressful the environment of each nation is and how the level of stress impacts the level of emotional investment in that country. One measure of stress they used was the Human Development Index (HDI), provided by the United Nations. This index takes into account the resources, education, and availability of health care in countries. There was indeed a positive correlation ($r[44] = .31$, $p < .05$) between emotional investment and the HDI, meaning that the more developed (or less stressful) nations exhibited higher levels of emotional investment than nations with a more stressful environment. The researchers also examined the connection between various other indicators and emotional investment. There was a positive correlation between gross domestic product and emotional investment, although it did not reach statistical significance. Indices that indicated levels of stress, such as infant mortality, childhood malnutrition, and the number of pathogens to which people are exposed in their environment, were negatively linked to emotional investment. Within countries, people from higher socioeconomic classes showed higher levels of emotional investment than people from lower socioeconomic classes (Schmitt et al., 2009).

Lower emotional investment levels among women were associated with higher fertility levels, as expected according to the BSD model. However, *higher* levels of emotional investment turned out to be positively related to the divorce rate in a country ($r[22] = .52, p < .01$) as well as to short-term mating interests ($r[41] = .44, p < .01$) and the tendency to engage with someone else's partner in a short-term affair ($r[4] = .55, p < .001$). With these results taken into account, the BSD model received only weak support from the data of the study.

There were also clear associations between attachment styles and emotional investment. Secure attachment was associated with higher levels of emotional investment, whereas preoccupied attachment in both genders (wanting to be close to others but worrying that one is not valued enough) and fearful attachment in women (wanting to be close to others but having difficulty trusting them completely) were associated with lower levels of emotional attachment. The eight nations with the lowest emotional investment levels had higher levels of preoccupied romantic attachment compared with the other nations in the study. Those eight countries were Taiwan, Morocco, Ethiopia, Indonesia, South Korea, Japan, Hong Kong, and Tanzania.

Overall, the study confirmed hypotheses derived from evolutionary theory suggesting that people from countries with higher levels of stress are more likely to develop insecure attachment styles and as a result have lower levels of emotional investment.

THE IMPACT OF NUMBER OF CHILDREN ON MARITAL SATISFACTION ACROSS CULTURES

Once people have fallen in love and also have decided to stay together and get married, they settle down and often start a family. What happens to their relationship at that point? And does culture have an impact on how happy married couples with children are?

CHAPTER 4

In the United States, having children stabilizes a couple's marriage. Evolutionally, this makes sense, given that parents of human young have to take care of them for such a long time. Puzzlingly, however, is that having children also reduces marital satisfaction. Generally, the arrival of a new child in a family can lead to conflict in a couple's relationship. But often, the child does not create a new set of conflicts; rather, the arrival of the child exacerbates the conflicts that are lingering below the surface. A study by Wendorf, Lucas, Imamoglu, Weisfeld, and Weisfeld (2001) set out to investigate these issues.

About 2,000 married couples from the United States, Great Britain, and Turkey participated in the study. Generally, husbands were a bit older than their wives and the couples were married on average for more than 11 years. On average, they also had more than one child. The authors found that, for couples in the United States and Great Britain, the number of children indeed has a significant negative impact on marital satisfaction. They found an effect of similar magnitude for husbands in Turkey. This effect was not significant, however, for Turkish wives, in whom they found only a very small, nonsignificant effect. It is possible that the small effect for Turkish wives is due to the fact that they live in a more collectivistic culture in which women are associated with family and motherhood. In fact, the Turkish word *aile* refers to both the family and the wife (Imamoglu, 2004). The length of the marriage had a negative impact on satisfaction as well. Since partners get older as their marriage progresses, the researchers also investigated whether the current ages of the partners affected marital satisfaction. They found that in neither culture did the wife's age have a significant impact on husbands' or wives' satisfaction with their marriages. The husband's age did have an impact on marital satisfaction, however. In Great Britain and the United States, older husbands and their wives were more satisfied with their marriages; this effect was independent of the length of their marriage or number of children. In Turkey, the opposite could be observed: Turkish wives with older husbands were less happy in their marriages. This may have to do with modernizing trends in Turkey and the likelihood that younger husbands are more egalitarian than older husbands. From an evolutionary standpoint, it is perplexing that the number of children would have a negative impact on marital satisfaction because the more children a couple have, the more important it is that they stay together so they can successfully raise their children. While there is at this time no clear way to explain this paradox, the authors of the study suspect that marriages are concurrently reinforced by the appeal of the children.

To summarize, culture interacts with relationships. For example, individuals in collectivist cultures have more close interconnections outside the family, and these interconnections can facilitate or destroy a relationship. In individualistic cultures, external relationships tend to be less important. But couples in individualistic societies may find that they lack the social support network available in more collectivistic cultures. Overall, one cannot fully understand intimate relationships without understanding the cultural context in which they are embedded.

A Primer on Methods: Constructing a Love Scale

In this book I have described a variety of love scales. How does a love researcher go from having a conception or even a theory of love to actually constructing a love scale? There is nothing magical about it. In this chapter, I will show you the inside workings of such scale construction. The example that will guide us is Sternberg's triangular theory of love (see Chapter 3). This will allow you to get a better grasp of how, in general, investigators transition from theory to practice—in this case, from a theory of love to measuring love as characterized by that theory.

Why do investigators construct love scales? There are several reasons.

1. *A love scale provides a way to test the validity of a theory.* Psychology is an empirical science. Investigators not only propose ideas; they also test those ideas. If an investigator has a theory of love, he or she needs a way to "operationalize" that theory—to conduct measurements based on the theory. A love scale provides a way to conduct such measurements and thus test the theory.
2. *A love scale enables people to assess how and how much they love other people.* Do you ever wonder how much you love another person? A love scale provides a way to get a sense of how much love you are experiencing toward another, at least in comparison with the feelings of other people toward their loved ones. In the case of some theories, such as the triangular theory of love (Sternberg, 1986, 2006), it also can give you a sense of how much of each of the various components of love you experience. That is, it helps you discern the pattern in your love relationship. For example, are you higher in intimacy than in passion, or vice versa? How much commitment do you have in comparison with your level of intimacy?
3. *A love scale enables couples to assess one aspect of their compatibility.* As you may recall from Chapter 3, partners tend to be more satisfied in their relationships, on average, when they experience (a) greater amounts of intimacy, passion, and commitment, and (b) more closely matching levels of intimacy, passion, and commitment. For example, a couple is likely to be a better match if intimacy is more important, and passion less important, to each of them than if one values intimacy highly but not passion, and the other values passion highly but not intimacy.
4. *A love scale provides individuals and couples an opportunity to enhance their love relationships.* Once an individual or couple has diagnosed a pattern of love, it is possible to use this information to improve the relationship. For example, if the couple is low in intimacy, they may wish to think about how to

enhance their mutual trust and capacity for self-disclosure. If they are low in passion, they may want to think about how to put excitement into their relationship. Just as doctors make diagnoses to prescribe remedies, we can all make our own diagnoses to serve as a basis for remediating aspects of a relationship with which we are less than fully satisfied.

The one important thing to remember is that as measuring instruments love scales are far from perfect. They can give individuals or couples a sense of where they stand according to the specifications of a particular theory. But this sense is only approximate and, moreover, ephemeral. Love is not a fixed entity; it waxes and wanes. So no matter how accurate a given measuring instrument is, it can only measure what a person feels in a given time and place. Moreover, the result is approximate and subject to measurement error: No scale is perfect. The measurement is also subject to the constraints of a particular theory. A scale based on a different theory might give a very different result subject to a different interpretation. Thus, love scales must be interpreted with caution and with allowance for the limitations of all such measurements, which at best are approximations.

As we discuss how to construct a love scale, you might find it useful to refer to the Triangular Love Scale, which is shown in Table 5.1. This scale is referred to a number of times in the discussion that follows.

STEPS IN CONSTRUCTING AND ASSESSING A LOVE SCALE

There are a number of steps involved in constructing and assessing a love scale. Sometimes the assessment is referred to as a construct validation—an assessment of the extent to which an

CHAPTER 5

TABLE 5.1   ITEMS FROM THE STERNBERG TRIANGULAR LOVE SCALE

Please rate your answer to each of the following statements on a 1 to 9 scale, where 1 (low) means that the statement does not characterize your relationship at all well, whereas 9 (high) means that the statement characterizes your relationship extremely well. Intermediate values signify intermediate degrees to which the statement characterizes your relationship.

Intimacy

1. I have a warm and comfortable relationship with _____.
2. I experience intimate communication with _____.
3. I strongly desire to promote the well-being of _____.
4. I have a relationship of mutual understanding with _____.
5. I received considerable emotional support from _____.
6. I am able to count on _____ in times of need.
7. _____ is able to count on me in times of need.
8. I value _____ greatly in my life.
9. I am willing to share myself and my possessions with _____.
10. I experience great happiness with _____.
11. I feel emotionally close to _____.
12. I give considerable emotional support to _____.

Passion

1. I cannot imagine another person making me as happy as _____ does.
2. There is nothing more important to me than my relationship with _____.
3. My relationship with _____ is very romantic.
4. I cannot imagine life without _____.
5. I adore _____.
6. I find myself thinking about _____ frequently during the day.
7. Just seeing _____ is exciting for me.
8. I find _____ very attractive physically.
9. I idealize _____.
10. There is something almost "magical" about my relationship with _____.

(continued)

TABLE 5.1 ITEMS FROM THE STERNBERG TRIANGULAR LOVE SCALE (continued)

11. My relationship with _____ is very "alive."
12. I especially like giving presents to _____.

Commitment

1. I will always feel a strong responsibility for _____.
2. I expect my love for _____ to last for the rest of my life.
3. I can't imagine ending my relationship with _____.
4. I view my relationship with _____ as permanent.
5. I would stay with _____ through the most difficult times.
6. I view my commitment to _____ as a matter of principle.
7. I am certain of my love for _____.
8. I have decided that I love _____.
9. I am committed to maintaining my relationship with _____.
10. I view my relationship with _____ as, in part, a thought-out decision.
11. I could not let anything get in the way of my commitment to _____.
12. I have confidence in the stability of my relationship with _____.

You can score each subscale by adding up the values and dividing by 12. In general, and roughly speaking, scores of 8–9 can be considered very high, 7–8 moderately high, 6–7 moderate, 5–6 moderately low, and below 5 low.

instrument functions the way it is supposed to, measuring certain constructs but not others.

Step 1. Decide on a Theory

It may sound odd that, before you measure love, you need to decide on a theory. After all, when you step on a scale you don't have to decide on a theory of weight. So why should love be any different?

The first thing to realize is that all psychological measurements are based on an underlying theory, whether the theory is explicit or just left in the background. As an example, consider intelligence. Although we may talk about a person's level of intelligence, or IQ, there is always a theory behind the measurement, even if it is left implicit. Measures based on different theories potentially give different results. For example, are all of the items on the IQ test verbal, or do some have pictures? Precisely what kinds of items are included? Do the items on the test take into account the cultural background of the test taker?

Similarly, consider measures of one's personality. There are a number of different personality tests, based on different theories of personality. The results of the personality test will be very different depending on the underlying theory. A test based on Hans Eysenck's theory will measure extraversion, neuroticism, and psychoticism. A test based on five-factor theory will measure extraversion, neuroticism, openness to experience, agreeableness, and conscientiousness. Love scales are no different from scales for measuring intelligence or personality. They all are based on a theory. If you do not explicitly choose a theory, you are nevertheless buying into a theory, whether you realize it or not.

Step 2. Construct Items

Once you have decided on a theory, you need to construct your items based on your knowledge of the theory. Item construction is something of a hit-and-miss affair. You construct each item with the goal of measuring some aspect of the theory. But it is not until later, once you have begun to assess the quality of the scale, that you find out whether the items are measuring what they are supposed to measure. At this point, you simply try your best to be true to the theory and construct items that represent the theory as well as possible.

Step 3. Content Validity: Ask Experts to Assess the Items

Once you have a set of items, you may want to conduct what is called a content validation. This means that you ask experts for their views on whether the items are measuring what they are supposed to measure. It is useful to obtain the opinions of experts because they may see things you simply do not see. After soliciting their opinions, you may wish to add some new items, delete existing items, or change certain items so that they better measure what they are supposed to measure.

Step 4. Face Validity: Ask Laypeople to Assess the Items

For a love scale, you want to make sure that the people who actually take the scale understand and interpret items in the same way you do. Hence, you may want to assess the "face validity" of the items. This means asking laypeople—nonexperts—for their views on the items. In the case of the triangular theory of love, you might ask laypeople to rate, on a scale of 1 (low) to 9 (high), the extent to which each item measures intimacy, passion, and commitment. (You could do the same with the experts; see step 3.) You want an item that is supposed to measure intimacy to receive high ratings for intimacy and lower ratings for passion and commitment.

There is one very important thing to remember: The ratings you receive from laypeople (or experts) may not correspond to the actual empirical (statistical) properties of the items. These remain to be determined at a later step.

After assessing content validity and face validity, you have a preliminary set of scale items. You now are ready to proceed to more formal kinds of statistical evaluation.

Step 5. Reliability: Assess the Extent to Which Items in a Given Scale or Subscale Measure Consistently

Reliability is a matter of consistency of measurement. Consistency can be of different kinds.

a. *Internal consistency reliability.* Internal consistency measures the extent to which all items in a given scale or subscale measure the same thing. In the triangular theory of love, for example, all intimacy items should measure intimacy and nothing else; all passion items should measure passion and nothing else; and all commitment items should measure commitment and nothing else. Statistical formulas can be used to assess the extent to which the items in a given subscale are homogeneous, that is, measure the same thing. The higher the reliability, the better the subscale is. It is also possible to measure the correlation of each item, or its relation to the whole scale. Items that do not correlate highly enough with scores on the whole scale can then be eliminated or modified so as to achieve a higher degree of internal consistency.

b. *Test-retest reliability.* A second kind of consistency is test-retest reliability, or the extent to which scores on the whole scale, or the various subscales, are consistent across time. You take a sample of participants and ask them to answer the items on the scale twice, with the two administrations of the scale separated by a time period such as 2 weeks. You then look at the extent to which the scores are consistent across the time period. It is important to realize that no scale will be perfectly reliable across time. There are a variety of reasons for this. One is that every scale is imperfect. Another is that relationships change over time. Yet another reason is that the subject simply may be in a different mood on one day versus another. Higher test-retest reliability is usually viewed as an indicator of a better assessment.

Step 6. Internal Validation: Assess the Psychological Dimensions of the Test

Internal validation is accomplished through a technique called factor analysis, which is related to reliability analysis. Factor analysis looks at the pattern of correlations (degrees of relationship) between the various items on the scale. It will identify the underlying psychological dimensions of the scale you are assessing. For example, for the Triangular Love Scale, what you hope to find is that the intimacy items all measure one dimension, the passion items a second dimension, and the commitment items a third dimension. Factor analysis can also tell you whether the dimensions are independent or dependent (correlated). For example, do people who experience higher levels of intimacy also tend to experience higher levels of passion or of commitment? Do people higher in passion also tend to be higher in commitment, or are they actually lower in commitment? Factor analysis can answer questions such as these. In the case of the Triangular Love Scale, the dimensions are indeed correlated. People who score higher on any of the dimensions of intimacy, passion, and commitment also tend to score higher on the other dimensions.

Step 7. External Validation: Does the Scale Measure What It Is Supposed to Measure, and Not Other Things?

External validation involves assessing whether a scale measures what it is supposed to measure, and does not measure other things.

a. *Convergent validity.* Convergent validity looks at the extent to which a scale measures what it is supposed to measure. For example, consider scores on the intimacy subscale. Levels of intimacy should correlate with other measures of, and with behaviors signifying liking, trust, caring, compassion, and communication. So an investigator might simultaneously measure intimacy with the intimacy subscale of the Triangular Love Scale and observe a couple in interaction, looking for behaviors signifying trust, caring, compassion, and communication. The intimacy scale would be considered more externally valid the more highly it correlates with behaviors displaying intimacy. The Triangular Love Scale exhibits high convergent validity: The subscales appear to measure the constructs that they are supposed to measure.

b. *Discriminant validity.* Discriminant validity looks at the extent to which a scale does not measure what it is not supposed to measure. For example, the passion scale is supposed to measure the extent to which a person is excited about—passionate toward—a partner. It is not supposed to measure, say, the extent to which a person is committed to the other person for life. The idea is that it is possible to be passionate toward someone without feeling much, or even any, commitment toward that person. In a one-night stand, for example, someone might exhibit great passion toward someone else but experience no long-term commitment whatsoever. The Triangular Love Scale exhibits relatively weak discriminant validity: The intercorrelations of the scales (relationships among the scales) are higher than the theory predicts they should be.

Step 8. Standardization

The last step in the construction of a scale is an optional one, and whether it is employed depends on the use to which the scale will be put. If the test is primarily for clinical or other psychological use, then it needs to be standardized—that is, administered to a large number of people—so that normative (typical) values can be assigned to scores. For example, suppose you receive a score of

7 on the passion subscale of the Triangular Love Scale. Just how high is a score of 7? Is it higher than, say, the scores of 50% of the people to whom the scale is administered, or perhaps higher than the scores of 75% of those people?

Standardization allows the researcher to indicate just how high (or low) a given "raw" score is compared with the scores of the rest of the population for which the test has been created. Sometimes test constructors create percentiles, as discussed above. Percentiles refer to the percentage of scores that an individual's score exceeds. So, if my score on the passion subscale exceeds the scores of 75% of the population, we would say that my score is in the 75th percentile. Note that a percentile is not the same as a percentage. The percentile compares one's score against those of other people, not against the total number of items on a scale. For example, on an intelligence test, one could correctly answer 75% of the items, but that percentage of correct answers would give no indication of the percentile for that score—the percentage of people whose score that 75% exceeds. A score of 75% correct could, in theory, be in any percentile, depending on how hard the test is.

Standardization is somewhat time-consuming and expensive, and is most likely to be done if a scale is generated by a professional test-publishing company for commercial use. The Triangular Love Scale is intended primarily for research use, is not commercially published, and is not standardized.

When a test is standardized, the first step an investigator (or publisher) must take is to determine the population for which the test is constructed. Who are the subjects for whom the test is to be standardized? For example, the normative data or "norms" (such as the conversion of scores on the scale to percentiles) probably will be different if the test is standardized on college students than if the test is standardized on a random sample of working adults. The two populations are at different points in their lives and consequently may have very different kinds of relationships. It is important, therefore, that the sample that is chosen be representative of the population to which the test publisher or investigator wishes to generalize. The investigator or publisher also may choose to standardize the test for more than one population—for example, trying it out on both college students and full-time working adults, with separate tables of normative data for the two populations. But, obviously, the more populations on which the test is standardized, the greater the cost of standardization and, typically, the longer the standardization takes.

Ideally, all scales would be standardized, but individual investigators often lack the funds (and the time) to support the costs of standardization. It is typically necessary to administer the tests to large numbers of people, often of various ages. Moreover, the people to whom the scale is administered need to be representative of the population to which generalization is intended. For example, if the investigator wishes to generalize the normative data to a population of college students, the investigator cannot simply administer the scale to students in the college in which he or she happens to teach. It would be necessary to administer the test to students in a broad variety of colleges that, together, represent accurately the range of colleges that students attend. Hence, the investigator would need to select some community colleges, some public colleges, some private colleges, some more prestigious colleges, some less prestigious colleges, some colleges in the East, some colleges in the West, some colleges in the North, some colleges in the South, and so on. You can see why standardization is time-consuming and usually expensive. To be done properly, it requires an investigator or publisher to embark on a major undertaking. But the result is a test for which scores can be interpreted in a more definitive way than is possible if the test is not standardized.

CONCLUSION

No scientist today believes that it is possible to capture the entire phenomenon of love through scientific study or through scales that are geared to measure love. But scientists recognize that if we wish to understand and improve intimate relationships, we need to understand the love that underlies such relationships. One way of achieving this understanding is through the measurement of love. No measure of love will be perfect. But such measures can provide a basis for helping couples with happy relationships make them even better, and helping couples with unhappy relationships to improve or even salvage those relationships. What better use is there of the science of psychology than to help people to achieve happiness through their intimate relationships?

Interpersonal Attraction

he beginning of many relationships is attraction. People feel attracted to each other for one reason or another and therefore start a relationship, be it a friendship, a business relationship, or a romance. In this chapter we'll discuss what factors influence whether we feel attracted to someone. We'll see how being close to or familiar with someone may make you feel attracted to that person, how someone's being similar to you or liking you may influence your liking for him or her in return, and how personality factors and physical appearance influence your choice of a partner.

CHAPTER 6

PROXIMITY

In 1998, Meg Ryan and Tom Hanks starred in a movie named *You've Got Mail*. Their two characters fall in love through the exchange of e-mails, not realizing that they actually are already acquainted in real life and don't particularly like each other. You've probably heard of love stories like that. Nowadays there are also lots of online dating websites like eHarmony.com and match.com. Those websites let you set up a profile online so others can find you. You also can peruse others' profiles to find someone who meets your criteria, ranging from size and weight to salary and the desirability of future children. The dating sites have lengthy questionnaires that analyze your personality and attitudes and then introduce you to others who are a close match to you on these dimensions. Some people swear by these dating sites; others use them but never find the love they seek.

A more traditional and quite promising way to find love, however, is to look to your immediate surroundings. Often in life people make friends with those who live or work close by. This makes sense, of course, because these are the people who are easily accessible, with whom you talk often, and with whom it is easiest to make appointments for get-togethers. And it is from those friendships that love often develops.

Think about your own life. Who are the people you are friends with and have been prominent in your life? In your childhood, didn't most of your friends live close by in your neighborhood? If you are in college, even now that you are much more mobile, do you have a substantial number of friends who live in or close to your dorm or attend the same classes as you? It is likely that you answered both questions yes. And studies show that when you sit in a classroom that has assigned seats, you are more likely to make friends with those who sit close to you (Back, Schmukle & Ekloff, 2008).

An early study from 1950 shows that we tend to befriend those who live closer to us. Students were assigned to one of 17 dorm buildings at the Massachusetts Institute of Technology. After a while researchers determined with whom students had formed friendships. People were more likely to form friendships with those whose dorm rooms were closer to their own. The same was true for friendships across dorm buildings: Students had more friends who lived in dorm buildings that were closer to their own (Festinger, Schachter, & Back, 1950). So physical proximity does exert a significant influence on whom we end up liking, and maybe even loving.

FAMILIARITY

To understand how proximity influences whom it is we come to like, we need to take into account familiarity as well. Have you ever heard of the mere exposure effect? This effect describes a psychological phenomenon in which people prefer some things to others simply because they are more familiar. Zajonc (1968, 2001) presented the participants of his study with different stimuli that included foreign words as well as faces. Some of those stimuli were presented many times whereas others were presented only a few times. When Zajonc assessed how much his participants liked each of the stimuli, he found that the ones that had been presented more often tended to be better liked. And this effect also applies to your liking of people. Obviously, you are likely to see the people you live closer to more often and thus be more familiar with them, which in turn can lead to your feeling more attracted to them (Reis et al., 2011).

One study had several women attend a class 5, 10, or 15 times during a semester. They did not interact with others but just sat silently in class. At the end of the semester, students were given photos of the women and were asked how much they liked them. Not surprisingly, the women they had seen more often were better liked than the ones with whom they had attended class only a few times (Moreland & Beach, 1992).

Familiarity may play a role even where we ourselves are concerned. In 1977 Theodore Mita and his colleagues (Mita, Dermer, & Knight, 1977) conducted an interesting study in which they presented women with photos of themselves along with mirror images of those portraits. The women had to choose which version of their portrait they liked better. (Obviously, they did not know that one version was a mirror image of the other.) They more often chose the mirror image of their portrait, which is what they see of themselves when they look in the mirror. That is, they chose the image of themselves with which they were most familiar. When friends of the women were presented with the same photos, they liked the original image better, which is what *they* saw on a regular basis. So, on average, participants preferred the portraits that showed what they saw frequently.

There is one caveat, though. The mere exposure effect typically does not work for negative stimuli. While it does work with relatively neutral stimuli, being exposed to negative ones repeatedly does not make us like them more. So, unfortunately, you can't endear your boyfriend or girlfriend to your annoying habits just by exposing him or her to them a bit more.

SIMILARITY

You've probably heard the proverb "Birds of a feather flock together." Is that really true, or is it, rather, that "opposites attract" when it comes to relationships? As you will see, the research is actually quite clear on this matter.

Much of the research on similarity and its effects is based on the *phantom other technique*. Researchers first assess participants' attitudes and beliefs and then present them with data on another person. The participants are then asked how much they like this other person, based on the data with which they were presented. Of course, the data are not really about another person; they are constructed in a way such that the "phantom's" attitudes match those of the participant closely, slightly, or not at all. Studies have shown that people generally like those who share their attitudes and beliefs more than those who are different.

But similarity is a very broad concept that can be applied to almost everything: looks, ethnicity, attitudes, socioeconomic status, and so much more. Similarity is almost always good, although sometimes it is more important than at other times, and there is one case where it is actually detrimental. We'll get to that in a bit.

Studies have shown that when two people have similar personalities, they get along better with each other and have a happier marriage (Gaunt, 2006). This does not really come as a surprise, does it? When two outgoing people are married, they enjoy going to parties together and attending other public events in which they can meet numerous people. Of course, their fun together contributes to the happiness of their marriage. The same holds true for two introverts, who may enjoy being home alone with each other reading books or watching TV. This doesn't mean that people who are different cannot have a happy marriage, but in general, similarity breeds contentment.

People rate their first interactions with others as more pleasant when their personalities are similar (Cuperman & Ickes, 2009). For example, there is a higher likelihood that an outgoing person will enjoy a first encounter with another outgoing person than with someone who is introverted and shy.

The same is true for our attitudes and beliefs. When you talk about politics, religion, social issues, and the like, it's always nice when others share your views; doesn't this serve as a confirmation of your own viewpoints? Two people really cannot have too many things in common: The more you have in common with another person, the more you will probably like him or her (Byrne & Nelson, 1965).

People also often seek similarity with respect to demographic variables. When someone shares your age, gender, socioeconomic status, religion, or level of education, you have a base on which to build a relationship. But did you know that people are more likely to marry someone whose last name starts with the same letter as their own (Jones et al., 2004)?

Similarity is important not only with respect to traits and characteristics. It is also important for the conception we have of ourselves. If you aspire to be a great golf player or chess player, you may feel attracted to someone who is accomplished in the domain of golf or chess. There is a fine line to walk, however, because someone who is much more accomplished in an area in which you aspire to achieve may actually lead you to feel threatened rather than attracted. Attraction will be greatest when the other person is somewhat better than you but not so much better that you feel like a failure (Herbst, Gaertner, & Insko, 2003; Klohnen & Luo, 2003).

So there are many domains in which people can be similar or dissimilar to each other. Do you think there is one domain in which similarity matters more than in other domains? Is it possible that similarity in one area trumps differences in a lot of other areas? That depends on the people involved. What matters most is similarity in those areas that are important to a person. John, for example, cares a lot about religion. It is therefore important to him to have a partner who also values religion and who agrees with him on important religious issues. Peter, on the other hand, is also religious, but his religion does not have much significance in his day-to-day life. He could easily live with a person who does not share his religion. Peter is a big art fan, however, and he spends a lot of his time scouting for art in galleries and visiting museums all over the country. Someone who doesn't share his love of the arts would probably have a hard time finding life with Peter enjoyable. So where similarity matters really depends on a person's interests, values, and preferences. Differences do not matter much as long as one attaches little importance to them.

There is one area, however, in which agreement makes a real difference to a couple's life. Can you think of what that could be? What is an area in which couples routinely have disagreements? You guessed it: housework! Studies have shown that couples who have the same views on the division of labor in the household and who share chores equally are happier together than those who disagree with each other or do not share the work (Amato, Booth, Johnson, & Rogers, 2007; Hohmann-Marriott, 2006).

So far everything points to our liking people more the more similar they are to us. There is one exception, though. When a person is sick or mentally challenged, we dislike them more the more they are similar to us (Novak & Lerner, 1968). This is probably because we like to think of ourselves as invulnerable, and if someone who is a lot like us is suffering from an ailment, it reminds us that this could happen to us as well.

In the preceding discussion, when we referred to similarity, that similarity was measured by psychologists using questionnaires and other instruments that assess a participant's interests. However, in everyday life, people do not use questionnaires to assess each other's interests and values; they infer how similar they are to each other from their interactions. And as long as two people believe they are similar to one another, all is well! In fact, relationship satisfaction is related more to perceived similarities than to actual similarities (Selfhout et al., 2009). That is, as long as you think your friend or partner is quite like you, you'll be happy, no matter how many similarities the two of you actually possess. You would think that the longer you have known someone, the more you know about his or her attitudes and values. So it is rather surprising that even people who have known each other for years through friendship or marriage do not know each other as well as they think they do, and believe that they have more similarities than they actually do (Goel, Mason, & Watts, 2010).

Now let us turn to the things that people do not share, that is, to dissimilarity. Have you ever met a couple who seemed like they had nothing in common? Perhaps you wondered why they were still together and for how long they might continue to share their life. Well, for one thing, it takes time to find out how much you truly share with a friend or lover. What first attracts us to a potential lover is his or her looks. You can't determine quickly whether or not you share a person's worldview, but it takes no more than a few seconds to judge someone's physical attractiveness. And the more attractive we find someone, the more we expect that person to share our views (Luo & Zhang, 2009; Morry, 2007).

It also probably doesn't come as a surprise to you that people change when they're in a relationship. They may acquire some new interests or take up old, forgotten ones. They may change their views on issues or may even become more outgoing or more of a homebody as a result of being with a new partner (Gonzaga, Carter, & Buckwalter, 2010; Ruvolo & Ruvolo, 2000). And people even come to look similar to their partners (Zajonc, Adelmann, Murphy, & Niedenthal, 1987). Some of the differences between partners fade just because they interact with each other and share common experiences, but some of the increasing similarity is due to people's trying to adjust to their partners.

There are instances in which it is a good thing that two people who love each other aren't quite the same. People can complement each other in many ways. When you think of your own relationships—with your parents or your friends—you probably can come up with quite a few examples. One husband may be a complete bookworm, have a lot of theoretical or academic knowledge, and be able to organize effectively, but he isn't able to change a lightbulb or repair anything in the household. Here it comes in handy to have a wife who is not quite as academically oriented but is able to do some of the light repairs that need to be done in a household from time to time. Or think about the way some husbands or wives dominate their spouses. They are very assertive, make most of the decisions the couple has to make, and generally seem to be the ones giving the directions in the relationship. A very dominating woman does well to look for a husband who feels comfortable submitting to her. A study found that couples are indeed happiest when they complement each other on the dimension of dominance/submission but are about the same on the dimension of warmth (Markey & Markey, 2007).

As you can conclude from all the observations so far, what is important for couples overall is to be similar to each other rather than dissimilar. Have you ever thought about why this is true? Why should we be more attracted to people who are the same as we are? Doesn't life promise much more excitement and adventure in a relationship in which partners do not have all that much in common? One major factor is that people feel validated in their beliefs, and overall as people, when they are together with others who share their values or interests. They are also more comfortable being around others whose reactions are predictable for them and, at least to some extent, relatively understandable. And, last but not least, when you meet someone who is a lot like yourself, not only are you inclined to like them, but you expect that they will like you in return (Byrne & Clore, 1970; Singh, Yeo, Lin, & Tan, 2007). That is something the next section will cover in more detail: reciprocity.

RECIPROCITY

It shouldn't really come as a surprise that we generally like people who like us; after all, it makes us feel good when we're liked. This is also what studies have shown. One study used a confederate to work on a project with participants, and at the conclusion of the project participants had to fill out a questionnaire that assessed how much they liked the confederate (who they thought was just another study participant). Before they started to complete that questionnaire, however, the experimenter arranged for each participant to overhear a conversation between the experimenter and the confederate, in which the confederate either spoke well or not so nicely about the participant. As predicted, participants liked the confederate much more when he had spoken well about them than when he had been critical (Backman & Secord, 1959).

So far, so boring. Isn't this what you would predict? Here is where it gets a little more interesting. Another study revealed that we do not necessarily like those best who like us without reservations. Aronson and Linder (1965) conducted a study that was similar in many respects to the study detailed above. However, in this case there were four possible conversations a participant might overhear between the confederate and the experimenter. Not only were there conversations that revealed whether the confederate liked or disliked the participant, there were two more conversations—one in which the confederate first claimed to like the participant and ended up being critical of him, and one in which the confederate stated that he initially did not like the participant much but grew to like him over the course of the study. When participants gave feedback on how much they liked the confederate, it turned out that the confederate was actually best liked in the role where he was first critical of but then ended up liking the participant, rather than in the role where the confederate liked the participant from the start. This is probably due to the fact that sometimes when a person smothers you with compliments, it is hard to tell if he or she really means it; maybe this is just a person who likes to shower others with compliments. However, when someone is first critical of you and then changes his or her mind and appreciates you much more, you feel that this liking must be sincere and that you actually acted in a way that gained that person's appreciation.

PERSONALITY

One thing that many people say attracted them to a partner is his or her personality. And, of course, that makes sense. Although at first you may be attracted to someone's looks, at some point the interaction with that person will become bleak and boring if you are not attracted to his or her personality at all. In a study that was conducted in 1968, Norman Anderson gave college students a list of hundreds of different traits that could be used to describe someone's personality, like "friendly," "trusting," "clever," "admirable," "moody," and so on. He asked his subjects to imagine how likable they would find a person who possessed each trait they rated. Then he put all 555 of those descriptors in order, from the trait that made people like someone the most to the trait that made people like someone the least. Obviously, he found that people liked others who have positive traits more than those with negative traits. Some of the most desirable traits were sincerity, honesty, loyalty, and trustworthiness. Some of the most undesirable traits were cruelty, meanness, phoniness, and being a liar.

As you can see, it means a lot to us when others are honest and trustworthy. You don't have to be perfect to be liked by others, however. In one study, experimenters had students listen to tapes of other students supposedly participating in an audition. On one tape, a particular student did not perform very well. On other tapes, however, the student auditioned very well and showed himself to be quite competent. Those tapes with the competent auditioner had two different endings: one in which the student spilled a drink on himself, and one without this klutzy ending for the student. Participants were then asked to rate how much they liked the auditioner. It turned out that the best-liked auditioner was the one who was competent but spilled his drink on himself. So, actually, some degree of clumsiness can make you more likable rather than less likable, perhaps because it makes you seem less intimidating than a perfect person would be.

At least if you're a man trying to impress a woman, being smart is also a good thing. Studies have found that the more intelligent a man is, the more attractive women find him. Men seem to know this intuitively because they use a more elaborate vocabulary than normal when they are flirting with a woman (Prokosch, Coss, Scheib, & Blozis, 2009; Rosenberg & Tunney, 2008).

PHYSICAL APPEARANCE

One major factor in interpersonal attraction is how a person looks. In fact, it is the most significant factor influencing our immediate appraisal of a person. You do not need much time to assess a person's attractiveness: When you see a stranger, you can discern more or less right away if he or she is attractive (Willis & Todorov, 2006). When a subject met with a stranger only for a short time and then had to decide if he or she was interested in that person as a potential partner, it was found that nothing mattered as much as that person's looks (Luo & Zhang, 2009).

You probably have encountered a situation more than once in which you talked with someone else about a third person who you found to be extremely attractive, and you were surprised to discover that your conversational partner did not share your assessment of that other person's looks. While this kind of disagreement is common, there does seem to be overall agreement on what makes someone attractive when you ask a large number of people, and this agreement spreads across different ethnic groups within the United States and different cultures around the world. We'll talk more about that a little later. First, let's examine what makes people look attractive.

One attribute that apparently makes someone's face more attractive to others is its averageness. How can that be? Here's how researchers found this out: They used a computer technique to merge photos of different faces and had their research participants rate how attractive the resulting face was. That is, they had participants look at composite photos that were made up of 2 faces, 8 faces, 16 faces, and so on. They found that the more faces they averaged into the final photo, the more attractive participants generally found the face to be (Langlois, Roggman, & Musselman, 1994). This seems to be almost a cultural universal, characterizing other cultures as well, such as those of Japan, India, and Nigeria (Rhodes, Harwood, Yoshikawa, Nishitani, & MacLean, 2002). See for yourself. Figure 6.1 shows composites of male and female faces. Which faces do you find the most attractive?

One thing that happens with faces as you average them more and more is that they become more symmetrical, that is, the two sides of the face become more like mirror images of each other. Some people have one eye that is a bit smaller or narrower than the other, or perhaps on one side of the face the lips are pulled up a bit more than on the other side. The more nearly identical the two sides of the face are, the more symmetrical they are. People find not only averaged faces attractive, but also symmetrical faces. Often averageness and symmetry go together, but they do not necessarily have to. A face that is not close to the average but is very symmetrical may be perceived as attractive as well (Fink, Neave, Manning, & Grammer, 2006).

What is it exactly, though, that people like in others' faces? That depends first and foremost on the gender of the person being rated. In women, features such as large eyes, high cheekbones, and full lips have been found to be particularly attractive (Cunningham, Roberts, Barbee, Druen, & Wu, 1995; Jones, 1995). With men, there is less agreement on what makes an attractive face, but generally a broad forehead and jawbones as well as a wide smile are seen as attractive (Cunningham, Barbee, & Pike, 1990; Rhodes, 2006).

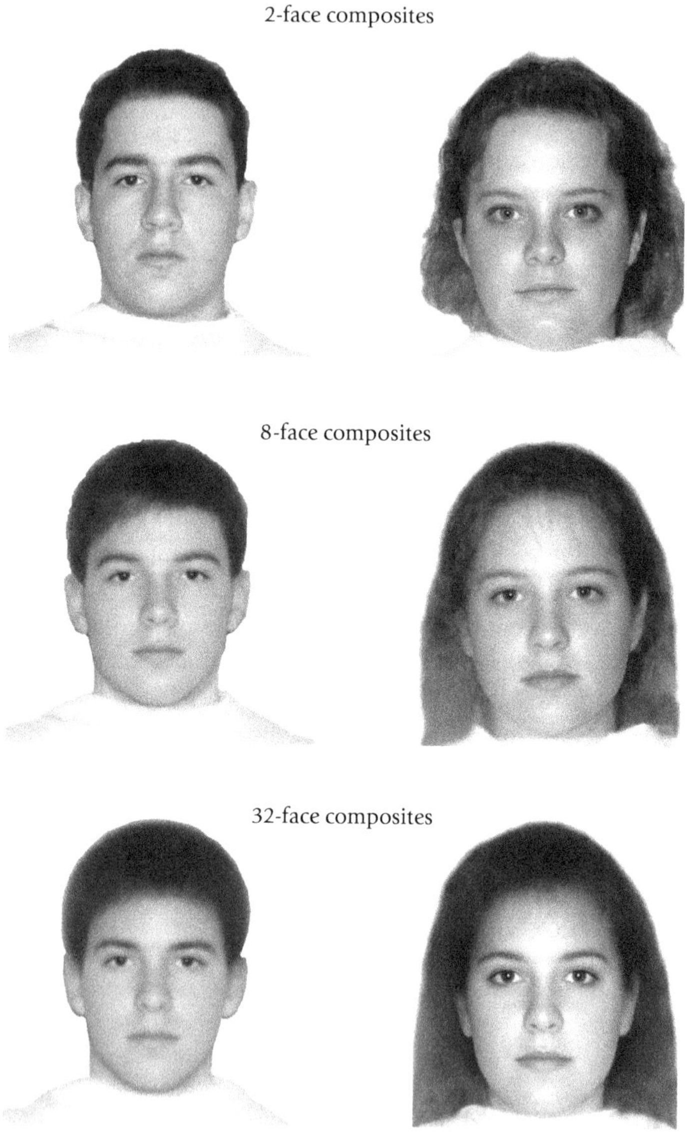

CHAPTER 6

2-face composites

8-face composites

32-face composites

FIGURE 6.1 Composites of boys' and girls' faces.
Source: Judith Langlois.

There is also general agreement on which features make a person's body attractive. Let's start with the women again. You have probably already heard of the waist–hip ratio (WHR). Men find it most attractive when the waist of a woman is quite a bit slimmer than her hips. A WHR of 0.7 (where the waist is 30% slimmer than the hips) has been found to be very attractive. You can easily calculate your own WHR by measuring your body circumference at the slimmest part of your waist and the widest part of your hips. Once you've gotten your two numbers, just divide the waist circumference by the hip circumference. Men all around the world prefer an hourglass shape in women, but did you know that even men who cannot see also prefer this shape (Singh, Dixson, Jessop, Morgan, & Dixson, 2010)? A study conducted with blind men (who obviously identified the body shape by touch and not by sight) found that they too preferred curvy women (Swami et al., 2010). Men actually are so much into the curviness of the hips and waist that when they are rating a woman's attractiveness, the WHR has more influence on the judgment than does the breast size.

Once again, things are a bit more complicated with men than with women. True to the stereotype, women prefer men who have broad shoulders and lots of muscles. If you're a man and haven't calculated your WHR yet, do it now because there's also a number for this variable that signifies what women like best: 0.9. In other words, women like it best when a man's waist is only slightly narrower than his hips. Actually, men with these features have sexual intercourse at an earlier age and with a greater number of women than do men who do not have these features (Hughes & Gallup, 2003; Lassek & Gaulin, 2009). Another thing that is very advantageous for men is to be tall. Both men and women prefer for the man to be the taller partner in a couple (Hitsch, Hortacsu, & Ariely, 2010).

It is not only a person's body that matters. Clothing can have an effect as well. People generally find strangers of the opposite sex to be more attractive when they are wearing red (Elliott et al., 2010). When women approach ovulation (the period during which they can get pregnant), they tend to dress in red more often (Gonzales & Luevano, 2011), flirt more with men, are more likely to slow-dance with a man in a nightclub, and are more open to casual sex than usual (Gangestad, Thornhill, & Garver-Apgar, 2010; Gueguen, 2009).

There are many beauty ideals that hold up in cultures all over the world. Someone considered beautiful in one culture is usually also seen as very attractive in other cultures (Jones, 1995). Looks may be more important in areas where life is harder and survival depends immediately on one's good health—for example, in many countries of sub-Saharan Africa (Gangestad & Buss, 1993). Someone's having radiant skin, shiny hair, and a proper weight almost immediately communicates, whether correctly or not, that he or she is in good health. Weight is an issue for which the value can shift depending on the circumstances of the times. When you look at baroque paintings, you will surely notice that the women are rather voluptuous. And, in general, larger women were the beauty ideal until relatively recently, when starvation ceased to be a major issue (at least in the United States). With the general wealth and well-being of the population going up, what is considered the ideal weight for a beautiful woman has gone down. Nowadays supermodels on the covers of magazines and in fashion shows are so thin that many qualify for the diagnosis of an eating disorder (Owen & Laurel-Seller, 2000). Some ethnic groups within the United States are a bit more forgiving of weight than others, however: Studies have shown that Black and Hispanic men are attracted to more voluptuous women than are White men (Glasser, Robnett, & Feliciano, 2009).

As mentioned earlier, we are very fast in assessing someone else's physical attractiveness, and that attractiveness plays a large role in our deciding whether we're up for a second date with that person if we do not know much else about him or her. Although we can judge beauty in a split second, it is much harder to assess someone else's personality and character in a short time. So by taking beauty into account, we have at least one criterion to help us decide about the desirability of another person as a partner. Additionally, we tend to assume that a good-looking person is also blessed with lovely personality traits (Dion, Berscheid, & Walster, 1972). And even though for women beauty does not correlate with the amount of time spent interacting with men, men's looks do matter: When men are attractive, they tend to have more interactions with women (Reis, Nezlek, & Wheeler, 1980).

So people react favorably to others who are physically attractive. Does attractiveness really buy attractive people anything, though? Research suggests that yes, it does. Because people smile more and have a more positive attitude toward beautiful people, attractive people tend to be quite sociable; after all, they have lots of opportunities for pleasant interactions with other people. This idea was actually tested in one study that had young men initiate phone conversations with women they did not know. However, they were shown a photograph of the alleged female conversational partner before the phone call. The photo showed either an attractive or a not-so-attractive woman. When the man believed the woman was good-looking, he behaved in a friendlier way toward her. Women who were believed to be attractive were friendlier as well, probably in response to the friendly manner in which they had been treated (Snyder, Tanke, & Berscheid, 1977). Careerwise, it may also pay off to be attractive. Attractive people are more likely to receive a job offer after an interview and tend to have higher salaries in their first jobs than do their plainer-looking colleagues (Frieze, Olson, & Russell, 1991; Hamermesh & Biddle, 1994). However, there is also a cost to being very attractive. With people being so friendly toward them, attractive people sometimes find it hard to trust praise from others because these people often bend the truth to score a date with their hoped-for flame (Rowatt, Cunningham, & Druen, 1999).

We have found that couples are often similar in many different ways. Does that apply to attractiveness? It does. While everybody wants the very best-looking partner, people usually understand that if they themselves are not highly physically attractive, they may not be able to get a date with an extremely attractive person. For fear of being rejected, they typically do not try to date the most attractive person around but rather focus on someone they think matches their level of attractiveness. This is called the matching phenomenon. Shanteau and Nagy (1979) express this phenomenon in terms of a formula that relates the desirability of a partner to one's attractiveness and the likelihood of rejection:

$$\text{Desirability of potential partner} = \text{Partner's physical attractiveness} \times \text{Probability of being accepted}$$

The higher your potential partner's physical attractiveness, the lower the probability of his or her accepting you. If that probability approaches zero, then obviously the desirability of that person as a partner is very low. Similarly, if the potential partner's attractiveness is very low, that person's likelihood of accepting you as a mate may go up, but the desirability of that person as a potential partner will still head toward zero. So, in effect, a person must find a balance between a potential mate's attractiveness and the likelihood of their being accepted by the potential mate (which is dependent on one's own physical attractiveness). This creates a similarity between the attractiveness of people who usually get together. But, as discussed before, other factors may play a role here—for example, someone may close one eye when it comes to attractiveness in a potential partner if that person is wealthy, famous, or influential in some way that is important to you.

Overall, when it comes to attraction, there are a lot of factors to consider. The most influential factor in beginning a potential relationship is doubtlessly physical attraction, which can be assessed in a flash and can serve as an indicator of health and youthfulness. Thus, couples are likely to start out on a similar level of attractiveness. Lack of physical attractiveness may be compensated for, at least in part, by money or fame. Of course, other factors, such as proximity, familiarity, similarity, reciprocity, and personality, play a role as well. But generally it can be said that a person prefers to get together and stay with a partner who is similar to him or her rather than with one who represents an opposite on many levels.

Stages of Relationships: How Relationships Are Formed, Maintained, and Ended

In this chapter, we take a look at the whole life span of a relationship. We start with a review of some of the kinds of love we examined in Chapter 3 and discuss how researchers understand the temporal course of those kinds of love.

Next we jump right into practice and take a closer look at a new way in which people are finding their mates: speed dating. Then we consider the effects of cohabitation on couples and what happens as these couples move on to marriage. We also discuss mechanisms that help or hinder couples in the maintenance of their relationships. Finally, we examine the usual means of ending relationships: breakup and sometimes divorce.

DIFFERENT KINDS OF LOVE AND THEIR DEVELOPMENT

As you may remember, we discussed different kinds of love in Chapter 3. Obviously, the trajectories of different kinds of love may be quite different as well. Let us examine some of those kinds of love in more detail and find out what researchers have to say about their likely course through time.

Consider these three scenarios:

- Larry and Ann have known each other for what seems like ages. They first met when they were on their university's rowing teams and were exercising together. Soon thereafter, the activities of Larry and Ann went beyond their rowing squadrons: They found themselves going to the movies together and helping each other study for exams. They never got romantically involved but have been close friends for years. Larry was Ann's best man at her wedding, and Ann helped Larry through a tough time in his relationship with his longtime girlfriend, which ultimately ended in their separation. They now live in different parts of the country but keep in touch by e-mail and occasional phone calls.
- Missy and Joe have been married for 7 years. They fell madly in love with each other when Missy interned at a local newspaper, where Joe worked as a reporter. Within a few months they were married, and for their honeymoon they took a 3-month trip around the world. Since then they have had two children, and Missy is currently a stay-at-home mom.

The passion they once felt for each other has mostly dissipated, but the two feel it has made way for a solid relationship that gets them through thick and thin.

- Alicia met Maria during a spaghetti dinner organized by the local church. Although Alicia is substantially younger than Maria, the two immediately felt like they were on the same wavelength. Soon thereafter Maria had a stroke, and she has been in the hospital for several weeks. She has no relatives who live close by, and Alicia is filling the role of family by visiting Maria every day and coordinating her medical examinations as well as following up on Maria's needs with her doctor and with the hospital staff.

Can you guess what kinds of love these scenarios describe? Have one more look at each of them and think about the kind of love you read about in Chapter 3 that fits best.

The first scenario describes companionate love—a friendship between two people who share interests and also share many aspects of their lives with each other. The second scenario is obviously about romantic love. That one wasn't too hard to figure out, was it? As you may also have noticed, the passion Missy and Joe once felt for each other has declined and has made way for a more stable, if less fiery, relationship. The third scenario is about compassionate love. Compassionate love also has been called "pure love," "selfless love," and "altruistic love," as well as many other things. It features prominently in religion as well as in literature about love, and often can be found in caregiving relationships.

Companionate love is a kind of love that typically develops relatively slowly. Think about your own friends. You probably did not become best friends with them within a day or even a week after you met. Instead, that friendship grew over time. Friendships are relatively stable and often endure over a long period, if not a lifetime. In Larry and Ann's case, you can see how their friendship grew over a long period, during which they shared

CHAPTER 7

both good and bad times together. All these shared experiences brought them closer together. And we can expect that they will enjoy their friendship for a long time to come, barring any significant events leading to a breakup (Berscheid, 2010). But things are not so rosy for relationships in general.

A longitudinal study by Hatfield, Pillemer, O'Brien, and Le (2008) revealed that, within the first year of marriage, not only romantic love but also companionate love declines. Thus, we need additional studies to find out if companionate love is really as stable and enduring as has been presumed. It is commonly believed that passionate love in long-term relationships may subside and develop into companionate love (Walster & Walster, 1981). However, there is evidence that companionate love is important in a romantic relationship from the beginning, and not just later on (Berscheid, 2010).

Now that we are talking about romantic love, let us consider what happens to romantic love over the long term. If you hypothesize romantic love to be a combination of affection and sexual passion, then it is reasonable to assume that if one of those two components starts to fade, romantic love as a whole will be affected (Berscheid, 2010). Ellen Berscheid (see Kelly et al., 2002) suggested that people in relationships have expectations regarding how their partners will behave and how their well-being will be impacted by a partner's behavior. If your partner does something that enhances your well-being, you feel good; and if the partner's actions decrease your well-being, you won't feel very good about your partner.

In the beginning of a relationship, you are more likely to experience surprises in response to your partner's behavior. Again, if the partner does something that makes you feel good or supports you, you will experience positive emotions; if the results of your partner's actions make you feel bad or interfere with your goals, you will experience negative emotions. The longer people are in a relationship, however, the more predictable the relationship becomes. These days partners' actions are rarely a surprise; people come to expect their partners to behave in certain ways, usually in ways that will enhance their well-being. Positive actions by a partner are no longer surprising and so no longer lead to unexpected feelings of happiness and bliss. Unexpected negative actions, however, still can surprise and can seriously endanger the relationship. That said, partners in long-term relationships mostly behave in expected ways, so intense emotions generally decrease as time goes on. Sexual intercourse also declines as relationships grow older.

As mentioned above, Hatfield and colleagues (2008) found that romantic love significantly declines during the first year of marriage. We can see some signs of this in Missy and Joe's relationship, where the initial passion has faded somewhat but has been replaced by what can be described as a solid friendship that makes their life together predictable and helps them navigate everyday affairs with greater ease as a result of the absence of the extreme highs and lows of passionate emotions.

Finally, let us consider the temporal course of compassionate love. It can develop quite quickly, as was the case with Alicia and Maria's relationship. A person can take an interest in someone else's fate within a short time and take actions immediately. A very important factor in the development of communal love is whether one person feels she can trust the other to (a) accept any support offered and (b) offer support if needed. Communal love is also part of a long-term relationship such as marriage, but conflicts and just the stress of everyday life can wear partners out and make them start keeping count of who did what for whom and when. If this happens, marital satisfaction usually decreases (Grote & Clark, 2001). There is not much research at this time with respect to the longevity of compassionate love and its development over time. The course a relationship takes may also depend on whether the altruistic acts of an individual are needed only on a short-term basis or whether, for example, a partner has gotten sick and will need intensive care for a long time or even the rest of his or her life.

CHAPTER 7

EXCURSION: A NEW WAY TO FIND A MATE—SPEED DATING

The ways in which we come to know potential partners have changed significantly in recent decades. In the past, people were often limited to selecting potential partners from the pool of people who lived in their town or area. They chose their partners from the people they went to school with, or the ones they met through work or hobbies. Nowadays young people can connect with many more people with a fraction of the effort that was once required. They have at their disposal a multitude of media to connect with others literally around the world. Think of the Internet in general, Facebook, dating services and websites, speed dating events, and the affordability of long-distance phone calls. Chances are you know someone who is engaged in a successful long-distance relationship that is facilitated by Skype, phone calls, and e-mails. And you probably also know people who have met their partners online, right?

One relatively new option for finding a potential partner is speed dating. For those of you who are not familiar with speed dating, here's a short summary of how it works. At speed-dating events, you meet with a relatively large number of people one by one for a short time each, just long enough to gain a first impression and decide if you are interested in the potential partner. Usually, people are seated around tables across from each other, men on one side and women on the other. Everyone is assigned a number. After a conversation period of three or four minutes with one person, a bell rings and the men move down one seat so that everyone has a new partner. The whole procedure is repeated over and over until every man has met every woman. The participants are given score sheets on which they can write down the numbers of the people they would like to get to know further. After the event, they can enter their chosen numbers into a system, and if a person they are interested in also entered their corresponding number, they can access their respective contact data so they can get in touch with each other. Depending on the event, you can meet between 15 and 30 potential partners in a single evening. In North America, the mean age of adults participating in speed-dating events is 33.1 years, with a standard deviation of 5.3 years (Kurzban & Weeden, 2005), meaning that about two thirds of all participants are between roughly 28 and 38 years of age.

One recent study investigated the results of speed dating in Germany (Asendorpf, Penke, & Back, 2011). Each event had an average of 22 participants. In all, 190 men and 192 women were involved in the study. After the event was over, a participant was chosen on average by 3.9 others. Remember, you only get the contact data for a person if he or she chose you in return. Each person had on average 1.3 reciprocated choices. About 60% of the participants achieved at least one match.

Let us first look at the features of the participants who were most popular at the speed dating event. Because no one has much time for conversation with any given person in such an event, you probably won't be surprised to hear that both the men's and women's popularity was based mainly on their physical attractiveness—in particular, the attractiveness of their face and voice as well as their weight and height. In fact, men seemed to use physical cues almost exclusively to choose the women in whom they were interested. Women used a number of other criteria as well to make their choices; they were interested in a man's willingness to have sex outside of a committed relationship (sociosexuality) as well as a man's income, education, and openness to experiences. What's interesting is that the cues women used in addition to physical attractiveness are all features that, as studies have shown, can be judged accurately even if you meet with someone only for a short time (see, e.g., Boothroyd, Jones, Burt, DeBruine, & Perret, 2008; Kraus & Keltner, 2009).

Unexpectedly, the more open men were to sex outside a committed partnership, the more popular they were with the women (although both men and women in speed-dating events generally are looking for long-term partnerships). It is possible that men who are more sexually oriented tend to have finely honed their flirting skills with women. In any case, shyness had a negative effect on a man's popularity, whereas shyness did not really make a difference to a woman's popularity.

As one might expect, the more popular a person was, the more picky she was in her choices. This makes sense because popular people have a greater number of potential partners who are interested in them, so they have a larger pool to pick from and hence can afford to be pickier. As the age of a woman increases, however, she tends to get less picky.

We discussed in Chapter 6 how people who have similarities feel attracted to each other. This similarity effect could not be detected in the speed dating study, however. The reason is probably that a few minutes of interaction is just not enough time for people to find out about their similarities.

Overall, the chances of finding a romantic partner in the speed dating event were about 5%. This may not sound like a high chance to you, but consider the likelihood of finding a partner when spending some time in a café. You probably have a better chance to find someone at a speed dating event than in a café.

LIVING TOGETHER

It has become commonplace for young people to move in together as a couple even if they have no plans to marry (yet). The number of young couples living together has grown significantly over recent decades, with about 7.6 million adults living together in 2011 (up from 440,000 in 1960, www.census.gov/population/www/socdemo/hh-fam/cps2011.html). Many couples who go on to marry have cohabited (Manning & Smock, 2002); in fact, about 50% of all married couples today cohabited before getting married (Bumpass & Lu, 2000). But most couples who live together out of wedlock do not stay together for very long: More than half of such couples dissolve their relationship within a year after moving in together, and about 90% do so within 5 years (Lichter, Qian, & Mellott, 2006).

Consider the situation of Jessica and Tim. They have been living together for about 2 years. They met at college but did not get involved with each other until after graduation. At that time both of them took new jobs in New York City, and they met from time to time since they were both new to the city and didn't know many other people. They were also both from small towns, and each could relate to the challenges the other was experiencing in moving to a big city. Soon they were a couple, and they got along so well that they decided to move in together—both because they liked being with each other so much and because it would obviously save them a lot of money having to rent only one apartment instead of two. Things have gone well for them, and they're still deeply in love with each other—so much so, in fact, that Tim recently proposed to Jessica. Do you think that their having lived together happily for 2 years is a good predictor of the stability and happiness they will enjoy in their relationship once they're married?

Many people think that living together with a partner before marriage is a good way of trying out their relationship to see whether or not it will work in the long run once they get married, but research actually casts doubt on this view. Many studies have found that cohabitation is negatively correlated with marital satisfaction and stability (e.g., Jose, O'Leary, & Moyer, 2010; Stanley, Rhoades, & Markman, 2006). Jose and colleagues (2010) conducted a meta-analysis in which they analyzed the results of numerous studies examining the effects of premarital cohabitation on the quality of marriages and their rate of dissolution. As predicted, they found a negative correlation between cohabitation and marital stability. That is, people who had cohabited were more likely to split up with their marital partners. A negative relationship also existed between cohabitation and marital quality. But why is there such a difference between people who cohabit and people who don't? Studies have found that people who cohabit tend generally to be less religious and less traditional (e.g., Stanley, Whitton, & Markman, 2004; Woods & Emery, 2002). Cohabitors also tend to have more negative interactions with each other (Cohan & Kleinbaum, 2002). Non-cohabitors, on the other hand, tend to be more confident about their future together and are not as accepting of divorce as are cohabitors (Cunningham & Thornton, 2005; Kline et al., 2004). Interestingly, the negative relationship between cohabitation and marital stability was particularly pronounced in the United States and may not be a factor, or may exist to a lesser extent, in other countries.

Cohabitation is a trend that is on the rise, and not only among young people. Older adults age 50 and above also are cohabiting more and more with partners to whom they are not married. In the decade from 2000 to 2010, the number of cohabiting adults age 50 and over more than doubled, to about 2.75 million. One big difference between older and younger cohabiting couples is that the partnerships of older cohabiting couples seem to be much more stable. When Brown, Bulanda, and Lee (2012) started their study on cohabiting older couples, participating couples had already been living together an average of 8 years. During the next 8 years, only 18% of the couples separated. Over the same time, only 12% of them got married. It seems that for more mature people cohabitation is an alternative to marriage rather than a precursor.

RELATIONSHIP MAINTENANCE

Once partners have formed a stable relationship, there's still a lot of work left to do. As you probably know from your own experience, relationships of any kind need serious work to keep them in good shape. At least in romantic love, where the passion typically wears off after a while, keeping the happiness and satisfaction partners once felt is not easy to achieve. There are different strategies and mechanisms people can, and often automatically do, employ to keep their relationship going. Consider what Lea has to say about her husband of 7 years, Michael:

> Michael is one of the most thoughtful and considerate persons I have ever met. He is always trying to make me feel loved and special, and is always looking for ways to make me happy. He is a great match for me because he has such a cheerful attitude and a great sense of humor. There are few people who can make me laugh as he can. And even though he is now in his 40s, he is taking good care of himself, which you can see when you look at him. Of course, he sometimes upsets me when he forgets to run the errands he promised to do, and he does forget quite frequently. But he is just a forgetful person and doesn't mean to annoy me. I try to be understanding. So overall I don't think I could have been much luckier in my choice of a husband.

Can you detect some relationship maintenance mechanisms at work in Lea's description of Michael? Lea has a very positive outlook toward Michael and their relationship. She mentions how Michael expresses his love for her through big and small things almost every day, and he shares in the routine errands that are necessary for their life as a couple. Lea is very appreciative of Michael, and she perceives him with some positive thoughts—possibly illusions—that make him look his best while minimizing his flaws. She also believes he is better than most men, and thus we can assume that she does not pay too much attention to the men in her immediate social surroundings who might otherwise seem to be attractive alternative mates. Let's have a look at these maintenance mechanisms in more detail.

Canary and Stafford (1992) developed the Relational Maintenance Model, which suggests that the type of relationship two people have and the degree of equity in their relationship influences what kinds of maintenance behaviors they engage in and how often they engage in them. They distinguish among five different maintenance strategies:

- *Positivity:* Partners have a positive outlook on, and attitude about, their relationship.
- *Openness:* Partners are willing to communicate and disclose information about themselves.
- *Assurances:* Partners express their love for each other and provide comfort in times of need.
- *Task sharing:* Partners share everyday duties and responsibilities.
- *Social networks:* Partners also have bonds with others, and value and share their social networks.

Edenfield and colleagues (2012) conducted a study that relates these relationship maintenance strategies to adult attachment styles. (Remember the different attachment styles we discussed in Chapter 2?) They found that people who are securely attached are more positive and open toward their partners and are more likely to give assurance to their partners regarding the relationship. People who are avoidant tend to distrust a partner's supportiveness and availability to them and tend to avoid emotional intimacy. Acting in these ways creates distance between the partners, which may exacerbate already existing problems.

Another thing that keeps people in relationships is feeling appreciated. A reason for divorce that is stated very frequently is that partners no longer feel loved and appreciated (Gigy & Kelly,

1992). Research has shown that when partners sense gratitude in their relationship, they feel closer to one another and are generally happier in their relationship (Algoe, Gable, & Maisel, 2010; Gordon, Arnette, & Smith, 2011). Gordon, Impett, Kogan, Oveis, and Keltner (2012) proposed a model that suggests that when people feel appreciated by their partners, it gives them a sense of security. When you feel secure, you're better able to concentrate on and perceive your own feelings of appreciation of your partner. When a person feels gratitude toward a partner and the relationship they have, the value of the relationship becomes clearer, which in turn leads to an increase in other behaviors that serve to maintain the relationship. The researchers conducted several studies that confirmed their model. When people felt more appreciated by their partners, they in turn felt gratitude for their partners and were happier in their relationships. Over the course of time, appreciated partners were more responsive and committed to their relationships than were people who felt less appreciated. Consequently, their relationships tended to last longer.

A person who is very committed to a partner also tends to think of the beloved partner in a particular way that helps the person stay committed to the partner and the relationship. For example, when the person thinks of the partner, the person sees him or her in an especially positive light; may see him or her as particularly smart or thoughtful, or may perceive the partner as being much better looking than the rest of the crowd. Even when the person thinks about the partner's flaws, the person perceives those flaws as less significant or less pronounced than the same flaws perceived in other people. Missteps the partner makes in the relationship are attributed not so much to ill will as to mistakes made accidentally (Conley et al., 2009; Neff & Karney, 2003). These interpretations of a partner's behavior and character are called *positive illusions* because the partner is seen in an especially positive light. Along with those positive illusions comes another perception, namely, that of the superiority of the beloved over other people (*perceived superiority*). And, as illustrated earlier in Lea's description of her husband, there is another consequence of seeing someone in such a positive light and believing that person to be so much better than most other people out there: If you are with someone who is so great, you automatically do not pay much attention to other men and women you may encounter. This *inattention* to alternative potential mates protects the relationship in that partners do not spend much time looking for other potential mates or imagine themselves in other, possibly superior relationships.

While there are many more things one can do to keep one's relationship healthy and happy, there is one last aspect of relationships that should be discussed in more detail: forgiveness. When people engage with others, no matter whether in casual encounters or in close relationships, they are bound to make mistakes sooner or later. And the better you know someone, the easier it is to hurt that person because you know that person's vulnerabilities as well as his or her strengths. People typically are hurt the most not by the remarks or actions of strangers, but rather by those of the ones that are closest to them. So in order to keep up a relationship, one must be willing to forgive a friend's or loved one's transgressions. Forgiveness requires one to let go of feelings of hurt and anger and to forgo any actions of retaliation. It is an active decision that one makes and it requires continuing work to be integrated into one's life (Hope, 1987; Waldron & Kelley, 2008).

There are three ways in which a person can grant forgiveness. Direct strategies require that the painful event be discussed; in such cases, the hurt person can even state directly that he or she forgives the transgressor. Forgiveness also can be granted indirectly by nonverbal behavior, including facial expressions. And forgiveness is sometimes granted conditionally such that it comes with some qualifications (Kelley, 1998).

BREAKING UP WITH A NONMARITAL PARTNER

Breaking up is always a hard thing to do, no matter how long you've been with someone. It is hard to hurt a person you love or once loved, and it is hard finding in your life an emptiness that once was filled by someone who shared that life with you. There are not many studies that have investigated the reasons why people break up with nonmarital partners. One study was conducted by Leslie Baxter in 1986. Baxter asked college students to describe the reasons why they broke up with their partners. All students who participated in her study were the ones who had ended the relationship rather than the ones being told about the breakup. There were some topics that appeared again and again in the descriptions. Participants described relationship guidelines that, if broken again and again, would possibly lead to a dissolution of the relationship. Some of these guidelines were:

- *Autonomy:* Allow and even encourage your partner to have friendships outside the partnership, to go out with friends, and to do things independently if the partner wishes to.
- *Similarity:* Share values and interests that are of importance to you.
- *Supportiveness:* Support your partner in his or her goals.
- *Openness:* Share intimate details about yourself with your partner.
- *Fidelity:* Do not cheat on your partner.

As you can see, there are some recurring behaviors that frequently cause friction in relationships. Even if a breakup was long overdue and ends a relationship that was not fulfilling anymore, and maybe hadn't been for a long time, there are many ill effects of a breakup on the partners. After a breakup, people's well-being is considerably lower, they are less satisfied with their lives, and they experience more sadness and anger (Rhoades, Kamp Dush, Atkins, Stanley, & Markman, 2011; Sbarra & Emery, 2005; Simon & Barrett, 2010). If you've been through a breakup yourself, none of this probably comes as much of a surprise. Throughout history, broken relationships have presumably always caused considerable distress in the affected people.

What has changed in recent years, however, is the way people go about ending a relationship. While most people still employ a direct approach and talk to their soon-to-be ex-partners in person (Zimmerman, 2009), a growing number of people are making use of the new technologies like e-mail and text messages. Weisskirch and Delevi (2012) conducted a study that examined breakup behavior with respect to communication technology and related the use of such technology to people's attachment styles. People who had attachment anxiety (i.e., they were worried about the responsiveness of a partner) were more likely to have been informed of a breakup by means of new communication technologies and also to use technology themselves as a means of breakup. Anxiously attached people may be particularly upset by the dissolution of a relationship, and their partners may be aware of this in one way or another. If the partners want to end the relationship but avoid a big emotional scene, they may choose to use new technologies as a means of dissolution. People with an avoidant attachment style were also more accepting of the use of technology to end a relationship. This makes sense, given that they are generally less willing to be intimate with a partner and to depend on him or her.

BREAKING UP IN MARRIAGE: DIVORCE

Dissolution of marriage has become quite common in American society—so common that the United States has the highest divorce rate in the world. In fact, it is so common that you almost certainly know one or more people who have been affected by divorce or have been affected personally yourself. Currently, more than half of all marriages end in divorce. Consider these statistics from the Centers for Disease Control and Prevention (CDC): In 2010 there were 6.8 new marriages per every 1,000 of the country's population. That same year there were 3.6 divorces per 1,000 (www.cdc.gov/nchs/nvss/marriage_divorce_tables.htm). The divorce rate of adults age 50 and over even doubled between 1990 and 2009, such that about 25% of divorces in the year 2009 involved people who were age 50 years or older (Brown & Lin, 2012).

There are marked differences in divorce rates between states. Nevada, Arkansas, Oklahoma, and Wyoming have relatively high divorce numbers, which hover between 5 and 6 cases per 1,000 in the population. Connecticut, New Jersey, Pennsylvania, and New York have consistently lower divorce rates, between 2 and 3 divorces per 1,000 in the population (www.cdc.gov/nchs/data/nvss/divorce_rates_90_95_99-10.pdf).

Most marriages end within the first 8 years (Kreider & Fields, 2001), but many people remarry quickly once they have divorced: The average time between divorce and a new marriage is not quite 4 years (Goodwin, Mosher, & Chandra, 2010). Generally, divorce rates are higher for those who have remarried than for those who are in their first marriage (Brown & Lin, 2012). This may be because when people remarry, they often have children from the first marriage, which may complicate the new marriage as a result of competition for resources and affection.

Reasons for divorce are obviously as diverse as the people who get married, but there are some topics that pop up again and again when people are asked why they got divorced. The issues leading to divorce range from infidelity and physical or emotional abuse, to alcohol and drug use, to people's growing apart or feeling incompatible with each other (Amato & Previti, 2003).

You may wonder whether the availability of the Internet has something to do with the rising divorce rates. After all, it is much easier now to find mating partners because people are not confined to their towns and immediate environs anymore. Dating websites and social websites such as Facebook abound, and they provide an almost endless selection of potential partners who may seem more attractive than the person one is with currently. Search costs for a new partner are arguably much lower than they were before the advent of the Internet. So make a guess: Do you believe that states in which a higher number of people have access to the Internet also have higher divorce rates? Todd Kendall researched this question and found that there seems to be no correlation between Internet access rates and divorce rates after controlling for other variables like household income (Kendall, 2011).

Interestingly, one factor that affects divorce rates is the occurrence of disasters. Whereas natural disasters like earthquakes, tsunamis, or hurricanes are followed by an increase in divorce rates in areas close to the disaster site (Cohan & Cole, 2002), human-made disasters have the opposite effect on divorce rates: They decrease them, at least temporarily (Nakonezny, Reddick, & Rodgers, 2004). A difference between natural and human-made disasters that may be responsible for the discrepancy is that the emphasis in the aftermath of a natural disaster is on the need to rebuild what has been destroyed, whereas in the case of unexpected man-made catastrophes, the emphasis is on the deaths that have been caused.

Catherine Cohan and Robert Schoen (2009) examined the effects of the September 11, 2001, attacks upon the World Trade Center on divorce rates both in areas close to Ground Zero and in urban areas across the country. In the months after the attacks, the divorce rate decreased not only in New York City and adjacent Bergen County in New Jersey, but also in Philadelphia and Los Angeles. No effect of the attacks was found in Chicago. So people in certain areas decided to postpone or even forgo a divorce after the September 11 events. Since New York City and Bergen County are geographically close to Ground Zero, it was expected that the divorce rate would go down in these places. Even Philadelphia is relatively close to New York, and one of the commandeered planes crashed in Pennsylvania. But the psychological sense of being threatened in an urban area is not enough to explain the drop in divorce rates since no such drop was found in Chicago. If you consider, however, that three of the hijacked planes were originally headed for Los Angeles, you can see how people in that city may have been particularly affected by the events. That means that the effects of a disaster can be felt even in areas that are not geographically close to the disaster area as long as the event hits close to home "psychologically."

The decline in divorce rates can be explained by Bowlby's attachment theory, which we discussed in Chapter 2. In times of stress and catastrophe, family members will stay close together because the closeness is comforting. No extreme life changes will be implemented, and the physical proximity will be maintained until the immediate threat subsides. So under the shock of the September 11, 2001, attack, people's first reaction was to stay close to their families for comfort and security. Consciously or not, people made adjustments in their lives to increase their chances of their survival and conserve resources. There were other, biological effects of the attacks as well: In both New York and Los Angeles, the probability of a male birth dropped significantly in the 3 months after the attacks. According to Cohan, this can be explained in terms of evolutionary theory, in that weak males do not survive to increase the chances that females can survive and eventually reproduce in a stressful environment.

But once people have divorced, what happens next? Are they unhappy forever and ever, or can they be expected to recover relatively easily from their divorce? Of course, when two people have been miserable in their marriage for a long time, perhaps for many years, a divorce can come as a relief. Nevertheless, a divorce is a traumatic event. When asked 6 years later if their divorce ultimately resulted in some good, however, about 75% of divorcees said yes (Hetherington, 2003). And, as mentioned, if people decide to remarry, the remarriage happens on average within 4 years after the divorce. Although good things can come out of a divorce, it is always a very difficult period for all people involved, and some will never be able to completely get over the trauma and stresses of their marital separation.

Online Dating

nline dating is becoming more and more common among younger people as well as older adults. It is certainly changing the dating scene from what it was a few decades ago. There is much buzz going on about dating websites. There even are claims about the Internet leveling the playing field between the more and less attractive among us. It is also said that people have access to many more potential dates than ever before. Some websites promise that if you fill out their personal profiles and questionnaires, they will be able to match you with others with whom you're likely to have a happy long-term relationship. But does online dating really work? And how does it work? We will consider these and many more questions in this chapter.

CHAPTER 8

HOW DOES ONLINE DATING WORK?

There are many different websites that people interested in online dating can use or subscribe to nowadays. Some of the websites cater to special niche groups, for example, people looking for short-term sexual encounters. There are also many dating services that aim at a large part of the population and try to distinguish themselves by means of the particular matching services they offer or by the number of potential partners people have access to through their site. What all these services offer to the user, however, is access to potential dates.

Throughout most of human history, until very recently, one's choice of dates was restrained by geography. You got to know the people who were around you and therefore eventually started dating someone from your immediate environment. Where you met others depended on where you went: You could meet your future spouse in a café, during a yoga lesson, at work, or on the bus to church on Sunday morning. But today people often feel restrained in their choices. Some people do not like to go out much or are too shy to talk to strangers they meet in public. Some people live in places where there they do not have access to a large number of potential partners. Some people feel that they don't have good chances with the opposite sex because their looks are different, and that meeting someone online first, where they can let their personality take center stage, would tremendously improve their chances with potential dates. Still others have not yet been able to find their soul mates and hope to do so through a special program that matches the personalities of people. So no matter what one's reasons for using an online dating service and what one desires, there is likely a dating service that fits one's needs.

Some online services are free and praise themselves for offering access to a large number of people. The website PlentyOfFish, for example, advertises that they have 50,000 new singles per day, and that more than 7 million conversations are taking place on their platform each day (PlentyOfFish.com, 2013). A Canadian website offers people three distinct categories under which to publish their profile, depending on whether they are looking for a short-term sexual encounter, a dating relationship, or a long-term relationship. Other websites offer matching services where the client allows the dating company to use data to match him or her with someone with whom the service claims the client is likely to have a happy relationship. eHarmony promises to match users based on 29 "dimensions of compatibility," with the goal of finding singles who are "truly right for you" (eHarmony.com, 2013).

But there are some general rules about how the online dating process works. You first select one or more dating websites offering options that seem appealing to you. Then you sign up for their services (which may be free or may cost a substantial amount of money) and create a profile that contains at least some basic information about yourself—for example, facts about your physical appearance such as height, weight, hair and eye color, skin color, and body type. It may also contain information about your interests and hobbies, occupation, and salary. Family-related information may be included as well, such as whether you're single, divorced, or widowed and whether or not you have children. When it comes to physical attributes, however, researchers found that more than 80% of online daters reported at least some inaccurate information. Most of those errors are relatively small scale and are not likely to be detected when prospective daters meet in person. Generally, men have a tendency to overstate their height and women have a tendency to report a weight that is less than their true weight (Hitsch, Hortacsu, & Ariely, 2010).

You also may be able to specify the characteristics you wish a future partner to have. In addition, you can upload one or more photos of yourself. This may not be mandatory, but people uploading photos have many more visits to their personal sites than do people who do not upload any photos (Fiore, Taylor, Mendelsohn, & Hearst, 2008). If the dating service you're using is one that specializes in giving people access to others interested in taking up a relationship, then you will be given the chance to browse the profiles. One study found that users spend on average more than 5 hours a week browsing profiles (Frost, Chance, Norton, & Ariely, 2008). You can filter the results by many different categories, such as age, relationship status, and hobbies. When you have found someone you are interested in, you can contact the individual through the dating website. How you contact and communicate with others through the site depends on the service you are using. Some websites allow you to send someone a virtual "wink" or write them a personal message. On some websites you can communicate via Instant Messenger (IM). Other sites have a system similar to e-mail. You may be able to chat with a prospect or even have some video conversations. And, of course, other people can contact you if they view your profile and are interested in you. You can either reply to their contact attempt if you're interested as well, and if you are not interested you can ignore it, send a freely formulated message saying that you are not interested, or click the "No thanks" button that some websites offer. From then on, it's up to you what to make of your newfound contacts.

If you subscribe to a site that offers matching services, then you may be able to browse only a limited selection of profiles that the company has decided constitute a good fit to you based on their matching algorithm. Those algorithms differ from company to company and are proprietary information; that is, the companies do not grant public access to them. eHarmony is one company that specializes in matching. They have you complete a profile that assesses 29 different dimensions on the basis of which they match you with others. The company groups those dimensions into core traits, which purportedly remain stable throughout a lifetime, and vital attributes, which are based on learning experiences and therefore can change. The four core trait groups are as follows (eHarmony.com, 2013):

- *Emotional temperament:* Self-concept, emotional status, energy, passion
- *Social style:* Character, kindness, dominance, sociability, autonomy, adaptability
- *Cognitive mode:* Intellect, curiosity, humor, artistic passion
- *Physicality:* Energy, passion, vitality; security, industry, appearance

The three vital attributes are

- *Relationship skills:* Communication style, emotion management, conflict resolution
- *Values and beliefs:* Spirituality, family goals, traditionalism, ambition, altruism
- *Key experiences:* Family background, family status, education

On its website eHarmony professes to match "singles based on a deeper level of compatibility, not likes and dislikes, but true compatibility" (eHarmony.com, 2013). This compatibility is supposed to help you find a companion with whom you are likely to have a successful romantic relationship for many years to come. Several services use matching algorithms based on psychological constructs similar to those used by eHarmony, but there are also other approaches to matching on the Web. An example is the one offered by Chemistry, which is based on a theory of Helen Fisher and allegedly uses sex hormones and neurotransmitters as a means to group people into four distinct groups, which are then matched based on compatibility. In addition, there are biological approaches that can be used

CHAPTER 8

as a complement to dating websites and are often integrated into these sites. To see if you and a potential partner are genetically compatible, for example, the company GenePartner offers genetic testing, which it claims should result in (a) an increased likelihood of forming an enduring and successful relationship, (b) a more satisfying sex life, and (c) higher fertility rates (GenePartner.com, 2013).

HOW IS ONLINE DATING DIFFERENT FROM CONVENTIONAL DATING?

Obviously there are quite a few differences between online dating and conventional dating. When you sign up for online dating, you have access to a larger, and sometimes substantially larger, pool of potential dates than if you were to go out in your hometown and meet people. Some online dating websites have millions of members whose profiles you can browse. At the time I am writing this, there are more than 500,000 singles online on the website of PlentyOfFish alone.

When you engage in online dating, you are able to prescreen your partners in a way you cannot in the offline world. Before contacting anyone, you can prescreen potential dates to match your preferences with respect to such parameters as ideal family size, attitudes and interests, salary, education, and much more. All of the things you can learn about someone else only bit by bit in the real world you can prescreen in the virtual world of the Internet. And once you have decided on whom to contact, the ways of getting in touch differ as well. With the click of your mouse you can send them a personal message. You may also be able to send IM messages or initiate video chats. Often people move their conversations off the dating website relatively quickly and converse by e-mail or phone to get to know each other better.

Once they reach the point where they meet each other in person, the differences between online dating and dating the conventional way begin to disappear.

IS ONLINE DATING BETTER THAN CONVENTIONAL DATING?

Now that we have considered how online dating works and how it is different from meeting potential dates in the conventional way, let us explore the question of whether online dating really works better for most people than conventional dating. One of the biggest differences is that instead of being restricted to the people in your immediate environment, you have access to thousands, if not millions, of other singles. Does having such a large number of choices lead people to make better decisions or give someone a better chance of finding his or her soul mate? When you are confronted with many different profiles from which you must choose whom to contact, you end up comparing your potential dates side by side. This is different from meeting someone in whom you may be interested in a bar because you probably would not compare that person directly with someone else. Rather, you would just try to get to know that person and find out whether he or she may be what you are looking for in a partner. In comparing profiles, a danger is that people concentrate on easily searchable characteristics and features they think are important in a partner. However, the characteristics they are most likely to weigh when comparing profiles may not be the ones that really matter the most when it comes to starting and maintaining a satisfying relationship. In fact, studies have shown that people often are not able to tell which factors will most influence their happiness (see, e.g., Dunn, Wilson, & Gilbert, 2003). It is also hard to get a grasp of more experiential features a person may have, such as humor. Even if someone indicates in his profile that he is a humorous person, people have different concepts of humor, and what one person finds funny another might not find funny at all. You can tell relatively easily if a person shares your idea of humor when you meet face to face, but online it is difficult to tell. Ultimately, when online daters evaluate many people side by side, they likely use different decision criteria than when they meet someone in a bar, and there is a chance they will not use the criteria that are most likely to lead to happiness later on in a relationship (Finkel, Eastwick, Karney, Reis, & Sprecher, 2012).

Some dating websites, particularly ones that offer matching services, may provide access to only a very limited number of potential dates. Part of the appeal of online dating for many people is that they have access to a very large number of other singles. When they are confronted with so many profiles, however, they may suffer from information overload because it is a time-consuming effort to browse through so many options and skim profiles that contain a large number of facts about each potential date. This may lead online daters to shut down cognitively at some point and lose interest in the face of so many different options (Iyengar & Lepper, 2000). Having such a large set of options to choose from may also make it harder to be happy when starting a relationship with someone. Research has shown that someone who is looking for alternative dating partners after starting a relationship tends to have a lower level of commitment to the relationship and is more likely to break up with the current partner (Le, Dove, Agnew, Korn, & Mutso, 2010). In contrast, people who believe they do not have many options and who feel that their access to a pool of potential partners is limited are more likely to view potential partners through rose-colored lenses (Gladue & Delaney, 1990).

Once the date seeker has chosen to focus on one or several of the people identified online, the process of communicating with them electronically begins. This process again differs from the immediate face-to-face communication with a potential future partner that is possible in offline dating. Research has found that computer-mediated communication (CMC) can be quite effective, and because there may be fewer social cues that can be communicated through CMC, people may even disclose personal information faster than they would in a face-to-face conversation (Reis & Shaver, 1988). If there are any gaps in the conversation that need to be filled through interpretation, online daters will often assume the best. Their hopes and optimism for a potential new relationship will shine through, and chances are increased that they will perceive the person they're communicating with in a positive light. Most people meet each other face to face within a week of having initiated CMC (Whitty & Carr, 2006). When the interaction moves offline that quickly, it certainly does not hinder and may even support the relationship by helping to build up intimacy quickly. Moreover, if people keep their communications restricted to the online medium for too long, they may develop false expectations and will inevitably be disappointed when they finally meet in person. Despite all of the advances in the digital realm, there are still some things that cannot be assessed in any way other than being with someone face to face. These include an overall impression of the person, the feeling that one "clicks" with the other person or does not, and sensual experiences such as reacting to the smell of another person (Finkel et al., 2012; see also Zhou & Chen, 2009).

Finally, of course, there is the question of whether the matching processes employed by various websites really work. It is hard to evaluate any matching algorithm because these algorithms are considered proprietary information by the companies that own the dating websites and are therefore not shared with researchers or the public. Finkel and his colleagues (2012) suggest that there are three general categories of variables that help predict whether a relationship will succeed or not. First, there are the individual characteristics of the people who are engaged in the relationship—their traits, attitudes, and beliefs. Second, there is the quality of the interaction in the relationship: Are the partners able to communicate effectively and do they support each other? Third, there are the circumstances that surround the partners and their relationship. Factors like unemployment, the death of a loved one, and disease are often out of one's control and can constitute significant stressors that put the relationship to the test. Obviously, matching websites cannot incorporate information of the second type into their algorithms because the partners have not yet met and the quality of their interaction is thus unknown. Likewise, many of life's circumstances will develop only in the future and cannot be taken into account by the mathematical algorithms as they attempt to match partners. What matching algorithms can do, however, is look at people's traits and try to match them for similarity and compatibility. A potential problem here, however, is that some people apparently possess traits that automatically make them better or worse partners, no matter whom they're matched up with. For example, people who score relatively high in neuroticism generally have a higher risk of a dissatisfying relationship (Bouchard, Lussier, & Sabourin, 1999). Also, people whose parents have divorced are generally at a higher risk of having a dysfunctional relationship themselves, no matter whom they are paired up with (Amato & Booth, 2001). But personality traits generally do not account for much of the variation in relationship satisfaction. Even neuroticism, the trait that has been studied the most and has been found to be one of the most significant predictors of relationship (dis-)satisfaction, cannot account for even 5% of the variance in relationship satisfaction (Karney & Bradbury, 1995). Thus, there seem to be people who just tend to have better relationships, no matter who their partner is. So knowledge of people's traits may be of no particular help in matching any of the thousands of individuals waiting to be paired with others on a website.

Many dating services promise to match people with others who are similar to them, but this approach is problematic as well. When lots of features are assessed and people's profiles are compared, negative and positive differences can simply cancel each other out (Finkel et al., 2012). Also, there is no general consensus on which dimensions of similarity matter most. In fact, the results of studies examining whether similarity between two personalities has a significant effect on relationship satisfaction are mixed at best (e.g., Gonzaga, Carter, & Buckwalter, 2010; Luo et al., 2008). The same can be said of compatibility claims. In compatibility, people search out others who have traits they themselves do not have. Say someone is a very disorganized person. That person may do very well with a partner who is organized and can bring some order into his or her life. However, research has consistently failed to demonstrate that compatibility contributes significantly to happy relationships (White & Hatcher, 1984). Thus, most predictors of the success of a relationship are unknown until the partners are together. What can be said for matching, however, is that some particularly poor matches can be weeded out so that a person can be presented with suitable matches. For example, some online dating websites bar users from participating if they show signs of mental illness or have been criminally convicted.

SAYING "NO" ONLINE

You have probably noticed that people seem to have fewer inhibitions when they interact online than when they meet in person, and that they tend to be much ruder than when they interact with someone face to face (Wall Street Journal Online, 2012). When people engage in online dating, they sooner or later will be in a situation in which they have to reject the request of someone for a date. Researchers wondered if date requests are rejected differently when they're made online as opposed to in person. After all, if someone does not know the person who is requesting a date, does not have to face the person, and feels much safer at home in front of the computer than if he or she were facing that person in the real world, doesn't that affect the way he or she will act? There are generally three ways in which a date request can be rejected online. First of all, it can be ignored. This is a time-saving way to say no that is used quite commonly on online dating sites. Second, many sites have a special "No thanks" button that people can click. Clicking this button sends an automatic message to the recipient that informs him or her that the date request has been rejected. And third, people can write their own personalized rejection messages, in which they are free to apologize, give reasons for the rejection, express concern for the feelings of the other person, and much more.

Stephanie Tong and Joseph Walther (2010) had 190 students read scenarios in which they were contacted by a hypothetical person who was interested in a date. All students had prior experience with online or e-mail dating. The presentation of the date request messages was either in the context of an e-mail or at Match.com. Furthermore, social distance was varied in that, in one condition, the person making the request was a current student at the same university who had once taken a class with the participant (low social distance); in the other condition, the suitor was an alumnus (or alumna) whom the participant had not met before (high social distance). Students were then asked to indicate how likely it would be that they would respond to the message and to formulate a rejection message. Participants in the Match.com condition were also asked how likely it would be that they would use the "No thanks" button.

Perhaps not surprisingly, when formulating their rejection letters, participants in the low-social-distance condition (i.e., the ones who thought the suitor was a distant acquaintance) were more polite than participants who did not know the person they were rejecting. Women used more words of encouragement (e.g., "I'm sure you'll be able to find someone else to join you for event X") and more often expressed their appreciation for the date request than did men. Apologies (e.g., "I am sorry I cannot join you") were more often used by participants in the high-social-distance condition. In the low-social-distance condition, students more often suggested that they stay in touch, however. In the Match.com context, which gave participants the option of a "No thanks" button, people used this button much more often when they did not know the person making the date request.

DOES THE INTERNET REALLY LEVEL THE FIELD?

When you go out to meet people in the real world, whether at a party, a café, a nightclub, or just a class at school, you make a first impression before you have opened your mouth to say something, if it even comes to that. People form first impressions mainly based on looks, and obviously the more attractive among us have an advantage when we're being judged without having been given a chance to present more of ourselves. Research has also shown that people ascribe more positive traits and higher intelligence to others who are attractive (see for example Eagly, Ashmore, Makhijani, & Longo, 1991). So, not surprisingly, a lot of people were excited with the advent of Internet dating because they assumed it would level the field between the more and the less attractive. The thinking behind this assumption is that when you engage in online dating, you do not meet your potential date right away; thus, you have time to let your personality "shine through" and to show what a beautiful person you truly are, even if you don't look like a supermodel from the runways of Paris or New York. However, is this really true? Have we indeed arrived at the point where superficialities like good looks don't make as much of a difference in dating? We consider this question next.

CHAPTER 8

Before we look at the impact of physical appearance on online dating, however, we'll consider another issue that you may or may not have thought about: the effect of people's first names on how they are treated in general by others and on their success in online dating.

When you meet someone, whether online or offline, one of the first things you learn about that person is his or her name. So when you start building your impression of that person, the name invariably plays a role. Research has shown that the impression a first name makes on someone can later influence broader generalizations that the observer makes about the name bearer (Nisbett & Wilson, 1977). First impressions influence later information processing, so how you perceive a person as you get to know that person better may depend in part on the impression he or she made when you first met that person (Kruglanski & Ajzen, 1983). So people with unfortunate names get treated differently, and mostly worse, than other people. They are subject to more discrimination and prejudice. Think about the endless teasing some children have to endure during their years at school when they have a name that lends itself to it. Not surprisingly, this bad treatment influences how people perceive themselves—their self-esteem and their self-efficacy (Leary & Baumeister, 2010). It can also influence habits such as smoking (DeWall & Pond, 2011) and hamper educational achievement (Cohen & Garcia, 2008). In fact, a study by Kalist and Lee (2009) found a correlation between the unpopularity of a name and juvenile delinquency. That is, the more unpopular a boy's name is, the more likely he is to end up as a juvenile delinquent. And this was found to be true whether a boy was White or African American. This study was conducted in the United States, and Americans may be interested in some of the names that turned out to be most unpopular: The bottom three, in descending order, were Luke, Walter, and Garland.

A study in Germany investigated the effect of an unfortunate first name on people's success in online dating (Gebauer, Leary, &

Neberich, 2012). Is it possible that people with less attractive first names are not contacted as often as people with more attractive names? To find out, the researchers tracked the responses to profiles of people with unpopular names on a German online dating website. They found that the effect of the name was actually quite strong: The more negative the name, the fewer views of the profile. People with the first name of Alexander, which is very popular, received 102% more visits to their profiles than people with the least attractive name, Kevin. This is in line with studies conducted in the United States, where it was found that job applicants with names that suggest an affiliation with being White received a significantly higher number of job interviews than did applicants with names that suggested the people were African American (Bertrand & Mullainathan, 2004). (We may not like these findings, but they are what they are!)

Now let's turn to the impact of photos used in online profiles. What kind of photo do people use to achieve their goal, namely, to attract a mate that fits their criteria for a desirable partner? To investigate this question, we have to distinguish between men and women, because the two genders have different mating strategies, at least from an evolutionary point of view. Women generally are a lot more picky when choosing a mate because they have to invest a great deal of time in their offspring. So they are best served having a partner who can provide for them and their children. If women engage in short-term relationships, they are likely to seek out a man they perceive as having particularly good genes, again to improve the outcome for their children. Men do not have to invest as much in their offspring according to the evolutionary argument. Their primary objective is to find a partner who is of child bearing age and who seems best equipped to have children and bring them up well. The question is whether these different goals are reflected in the photos that people publish in their online profiles: Since men are interested in fertile women, women should present photos of themselves that underscore their youthfulness, beauty, and health. And since women are more interested in partners who can provide for future offspring, men should post photos that depict status, wealth, and success. Serge Gallant and his colleagues (Gallant, Williams, Fisher, & Cox, 2011) analyzed 150 photos of men and 150 photos of women who were searching for a partner on a Canadian online dating website. One particularity of that website is that you can choose to advertise in three different categories: long-term relationship, dating relationship, and a category primarily for people who seek sexual encounters. Here are the results of the photo analysis: Women indeed portrayed themselves more often as smiling and in an indoor setting (to indicate their domesticity and ability to raise children). They also exposed more skin than did men. Women in the category for sexual encounters also wore scanty clothing more often. Men, on the other hand, more often showed photos that displayed them with a view from below in order to make them appear bigger, flexed their muscles more often in the photos, and displayed more gray hair than women did.

Rebecca Brand and her colleagues (Brand, Bonatsos, D'Orazio, & DeShong, 2012) went further than just investigating the impact of the photo on online dating. The researchers hypothesized that if it is true that good looks are assumed to come with good social skills as well as higher intelligence, then maybe the Internet doesn't level the playing field after all. Think about it. In online dating, photos are accompanied by profile texts in which people present themselves to anyone who may be interested in them. If people who are particularly attractive also tend to be more competent cognitively, their texts may be more appealing as well. If this is the case, the researchers should find a positive correlation between the attractiveness of the profile photo and the appeal of the accompanying text. To investigate this question, the researchers had 50 female college students evaluate photos and texts from a real online dating website. To make sure that the women were not influenced by the photo when evaluating the text or vice versa, they were presented with either the photo or the text of a man, but never both. The women had to judge the photos for physical attractiveness (overall as well as for purposes of a short-term sexual and a long-term relationship), kindness, confidence, masculinity, and symmetry. The texts were evaluated for how attractive the man seemed (again, overall as well as for a short sexual encounter and a long relationship) as well as for kindness, confidence, intelligence, and humor. The results indeed showed the expected positive correlation between text attractiveness and photo attractiveness (although the text and photo of any one individual were never judged by the same woman). That means that, generally, the more attractive the photo of a person is, the more attractive is the text that accompanies the photo. The texts were judged as attractive mostly when they exuded confidence. And, in turn, when the text conveyed a certain level of confidence, the photo tended to be more attractive as well. So the more confidence a man exuded in his writing, the more attractive women found his text and the more attractive they also found his photo. It is not quite clear why some men—in particular, attractive men—would be more associated with an aura of confidence than more average-looking men, but the researchers believe this may be because attractive men have a history of being treated relatively well throughout their lives and a resulting awareness of having a relatively high value in the market for potential mates. Thus, you can make an argument that when men are writing texts for an online dating website, they should try to sound as confident as possible. We do not know for sure, but it is possible that a confident-sounding text accompanied by the photo of a less-than-attractive man would not impress women but would rather make the man seem boastful and smug. So, unfortunately, it seems that even online, attractive individuals still have an edge in the competition.

CHAPTER 8

THE DANGERS OF ONLINE DATING

You may have heard about all kinds of scam artists who are trying to take advantage of Internet users. They range from the supposedly wealthy Nigerian family that needs the victim's help to transfer a large sum of money out of the country, to lottery scams where the victim is notified he or she has won a large sum of money but has to pay a certain amount up front to collect the winnings. Then there is the bank e-mail scam that asks you to submit your debit card number and PIN number online. In 2012, fraud loss in Great Britain totaled about 73 billion pounds, which is more than $111 billion. And the costs of fraud are rising steeply, reaching almost twice the amount from 2011, 38 billion pounds (National Fraud Authority, 2012). Scammers are quick to find new and inventive ways to make use of the latest technology to relieve their victims of often substantial amounts of money, and since 2008 this has included fraudulent activities involving online dating (Whitty & Buchanan, 2012). The scammer contacts his victim through an online dating website and establishes a relationship with him or her. This relationship can last as long as 6 to 8 months, during which the scammer tries to create strong emotional ties with the victim. Then the scammer comes up with a story of some unfortunate stroke of fate that befell him, such as losing his identification documents on an overseas trip, a sudden severe sickness, or some other cause of unexpected expenses. The scammer then asks the victim for financial assistance. Not only does the online romance scam relieve people of their money, but it also can result in severe emotional trauma to the victim from having been betrayed by someone with whom she thought she had a close personal relationship.

Whitty and Buchanan (2012) conducted a survey of more than 200 online daters and found that 0.65% of them had been scammed—which, if you extrapolate over the entire population of Great Britain, gives an estimate of 230,000 people having fallen prey to an online dating scam. What's more, 2.28% of respondents indicated they knew someone personally who had been defrauded in an online romance scam. This translates to more than 1 million British adults. So as people turn to the Internet to help them find the love of their life, it always pays to be attentive and to be wary when someone who is not personally familiar makes extreme claims or even asks for money.

Given the prevalence of Internet scams of all sorts, and the emotional vulnerability added to the financial risk of online romance scams, it is no wonder that Internet daters are somewhat wary of who they may be meeting online. Their concerns can be categorized as (a) concerns about lies and deceptive information, (b) sexual risks, (c), risks to one's affective state and physical safety, and (d) the risk of meeting deceitful people (Couch, Liamputtong, & Pitts, 2012).

Another study found similar concerns and also investigated what people do to reduce their uncertainty. Gibbs, Ellison, and Lai (2011) found that Internet daters have three prevailing concerns: that their personal security is at risk, that their prospective date is misrepresenting who he or she is, and that they may be recognized as dating online, which could embarrass them. To decrease their risk, Gibbs and colleagues note that daters can engage in several information-seeking or appraising strategies: They can look up their potential partner using an Internet search engine; they can compare e-mail or IM conversations for consistency or ask follow-up questions in e-mails or IM texts; they can ask follow-up questions in conversations on the phone; and they can compare photos of the profile of their potential date to the demographic and written information the person is giving. In the study, participants who used more of these strategies to confirm the identity of an Internet date tended to disclose more personal information and emotions than did participants who did not use as many uncertainty-reduction strategies. Some people go as far as checking public records, but the researchers found that most people just ask their dates questions in online conversations to find out more about them or compare information about their dates from multiple websites, such as other online dating sites or Facebook. Interestingly, looking up the other using Internet search engines was the least popular strategy employed by the online daters. In the end, the lesson is: When you date online, beware!

Love and Personality

ach of us is able to get along with some people and not with others. When we don't get along with someone, we may refer to our having a "personality conflict" with that person. When we do get along with someone, we might view ourselves as having "compatible personalities." Can we find out who might be a good love match by understanding a possible partner's personality?

SIMILARITY VERSUS COMPLEMENTARITY

The basic question in the literature on love has been this: Do we fare better in relationships in which we are similar in personality to one another or in those in which we are complementary—that is, different?

CHAPTER 9

Psychologists have come out on both sides of this issue. For example, Byrne and Griffitt (1973) have argued for the importance of similarity; thus, they are proponents of similarity theory. According to this view, if you are an extravert, then you probably want to pair up with another extravert. For example, if you like to go to parties to meet and interact with people, then you probably want to be with a partner who also likes to go to parties and meet up with others. If you get paired with a homebody who dreads the thought of going out to parties, and who would rather stay home and read, you are likely to become frustrated and eventually quite unhappy. Similarity theory does not apply only to personality traits. You probably want to be with someone who shares your interests, so you can do things together, and shares your values, so that the two of you see things the same way. If you have very different values—for example, one of you believes in being gentle with children and the other believes that if you spare the rod, you spoil the child—you may experience a great deal of conflict in raising your children. Even similarity in physical attractiveness may be important, lest one partner feel like the ugly duckling in the relationship and the other partner feel that he or she deserves someone more attractive.

An alternative view is called complementarity theory and has been proposed by, among others, Kerckhoff and Davis (1962). According to this view, partners will fare better if they are complementary—in other words, if they differ in key respects. Consider, for example, an individual who is extremely conscientious. Similarity theory holds that he or she would do best to partner with someone else who is very conscientious. But complementarity theory suggests that two extremely conscientious people might drive each other up the wall. Perhaps a man who is very conscientious needs to be with a woman who is willing occasionally to let down her hair. Perhaps a woman who is less conscientious needs to be with someone who can hold her feet to the fire. Complementarity theory does make some sense.

There is considerable evidence for the operation of similarity and very little for the operation of complementarity (e.g., Miller, 2012; White & Hatcher, 1984). In general, differences are associated with marital instability and breakup. However, another point of view is that the issue of similarity versus complementarity has been misdefined.

It is possible that the evidence for complementarity is weak compared with the evidence for similarity because the hypothesis has not been tested adequately. Consider an example of how the debate regarding similarity and complementarity might be refined.

In his theory of love as a story, R. Sternberg (1998) argues that we look for people who have stories of love that are compatible with our own. These stories are developed from the time we are very young, as an interaction between our personalities and our experiences in the environment observing love relationships—for example, the stories of our parents and friends' parents, the stories we see in movies, the stories we read about, and so forth. In some of these stories, the roles of the two partners are similar. For example, a business story involves two business partners trying to make a private venture succeed, a travel story tells of two people traveling together through life, and a fairy-tale story is about a prince seeking his princess or vice versa. But in other stories the roles are complementary. Examples are a teacher–student story in which a teacher instructs a student about life, a police story in which a police officer carefully tracks a potential criminal (such as a spouse suspected of disloyalty), and a horror story in which a terrorizer stalks a victim.

This theory postulates that simply talking about similarity or complementarity is naïve. Whether similarity or complementarity is a better predictor of success depends on the story. In stories where the roles of the two partners are similar, similarity should predict relationship success; but in stories where the roles are complementary, complementarity should predict success.

CHAPTER 9

Moreover, a given individual does not have just one story but a hierarchy of stories, with some more powerful than others. Thus, whether similarity or complementarity will apply depends on the hierarchy of stories for a given set of partners. In different relationships, different patterns of predictions might be relevant. One has to look at each pair of partners and the love stories under which they operate.

Consider Brian and Jean. They have a happy marriage, but is it because they are similar or because they are complementary? In their case, it is both. They have similar values and similar interests, which helps them when they have decisions to make and also when they look for things to do. They have similar expectations about the role of children in their lives and also about the role of religion. Both of them are relatively thrifty. These similarities help them get through the daily grind.

But in one respect they are very different. Brian is 15 years older than Jean and has been married before. He grew up in a large city and entered the school of hard knocks at an early age. Through his experiences, and from having lived abroad for 5 years, he has learned a lot about life.

Jean grew up in a relatively sheltered environment. She was raised in a small town, went to the schools in that town, and then attended a religious college where contact with people from the outside was not encouraged. Brian was her first serious boyfriend. So she entered the relationship feeling that she lacked the knowledge about life to be able to negotiate its many challenges successfully.

Brian, at the same time, felt he had the life experience to complement Jean's lack of experience, and he was and still is as eager to teach as she is to learn. In essence, theirs is a "teacher–student" story. They are comfortable with it, and with the complementarity of their roles. So Brian and Jean are similar in ways that lead to success, but they are complementary in one major respect, one that has also led to their success. Brian would have been unhappy had Jean not wanted to learn from him, and Jean would have been unhappy had Brian not wanted to teach her. They take advantage of their complementarity in a relationship-enhancing way.

Bill and Suzanne are also similar in many respects, and they too have one key difference. Bill saw Suzanne as the princess of his dreams. Suzanne was attracted to Bill largely because he is handsome but also because he has been economically successful and someone on whom she could count in times of financial need. She grew up dirt poor and has never forgotten the uncertainty with which she lived her entire childhood. She has taken pains to avoid repeating the experience.

The problem is that Bill and Suzanne, although attracted to each other, have clashing stories. Bill is looking for a partner with a fairy-tale story—of a prince and a princess—whereas Suzanne is looking for a partner with a business story—of two financial partners working their way through life. The upshot is that Bill finds Suzanne too preoccupied with money and Suzanne finds Bill to be something of an idealistic dreamer who she believes does not understand how the world works. Thus, the similarities between Bill and Suzanne, which are considerable, are not enough to make their relationship succeed, and they split up.

There is another theory of R. Sternberg that claims that one cannot compare similarity and complementarity views simply on an either-or basis. According to Sternberg (1997), people have different styles of thinking. For example, legislatively oriented people like to come up with their own ways of doing things and prefer to be given very little structure and direction; they sometimes rebel if they feel that they are being forced into a mold. Executively oriented people, in contrast, prefer some degree of structure and direction. They would rather have guidelines for the tasks they need to perform. Judicially oriented people like to judge things and also other people. They tend to take an evaluative approach to managing what they encounter in life.

CHAPTER 9

According to this theory, similarity and complementarity each have advantages and disadvantages in a relationship. For example, two legislatively oriented people are likely to find each other interesting and engaging. But if each of them wants to be the one who plans things out and makes decisions, the two may come into conflict. Two executive types may feel comfortable with each other because neither one has strong views about how things should be done; both look to outsiders for guidance. But the risk is that they will end up dissatisfied because no one in the relationship is taking responsibility for planning and guiding things. Two judicial types may have a great time chatting about their respective evaluations of other people, but if they start turning their evaluations toward each other, conflict will ensue if the other does not agree with the evaluation. In contrast, a legislative person and an executive person may make a natural couple because one tends to set the direction and the other to follow it. But they may encounter conflict if the legislator becomes bored with the executive, or if the executive starts to resent the legislator for wanting things his or her own way.

As an example, Beth and Marc have a very exciting relationship. They are both full of ideas about what to do and how to do it. Beth and Marc especially like to travel, so they are both thrilled with their shared interest and are continuously striving to expand their horizons. They have one source of fairly constant conflict, however: Beth likes to plan a lot of activities well in advance and fill every minute with sights to see and things to do. Her rationale is that their time for travel is limited and they should take in everything they can in what time they do have. Marc, in contrast, tends to be opportunistic—to go to a given locale and see what emerges. He actually prefers a certain amount of dead time on trips so he can feel that he has time to relax. He finds that if he and Beth are constantly running around, there is no time for them to actually unwind. Because they are both "legislative" in their approach to the relationship, they each want to have their way. Their common desire to set the agenda leads them to conflict and to disappointment in that no trip ends up being quite what either had hoped for. The similarity of their legislative styles leads them to conflict because they differ with respect to what they hope to get out of a trip.

In sum, the evidence suggests that similarity is more important than complementarity in most relationships. But have the theories been adequately tested against each other? An adequate test would have to be more sophisticated—looking at particular attributes as they apply to particular pairs of people—than a mere examination of whether, in terms of a given trait, successful couples are more similar or more different.

BIG FIVE PERSONALITY TRAITS

The most widely utilized theory of personality today is sometimes referred to as the Big Five theory (see, e.g., Costa & McCrae, 1992; Goldberg, 1993) because it posits that five overarching dimensions of personality dominate over other, less common personality traits, and that the five traits, if not universal, at least apply extremely broadly across people and nations. The five dimensions are agreeableness, conscientiousness, extraversion, neuroticism, and openness to experience. People who are agreeable tend to be easy to get along with, sympathetic, and interested in other people. Those who are conscientious tend to be exacting in what they do, sticklers for the details of assignments, and motivated to get things done on time. People who are extraverted tend to be eager to meet new people, comfortable at parties, gregarious, and easy to talk to. People who are neurotic tend to be easily bothered and irritated, prone to excessive worry, and generally moody. And people who are open to experience tend to be interested in learning new things, to seek new experiences, and to think in imaginative ways.

CHAPTER 9

As you might expect, agreeableness is positively associated with variables leading to success in a relationship, such as satisfaction and stability (Karney & Bradbury, 1995). If there is a risk with this dimension, it is that couples who are both high in agreeableness may avoid conflict even when a conflict is necessary to resolve an issue. Hence, it is important in relationships to strive for agreement and to be considerate of the needs of your partner, but also to ensure that when there are disagreements, they are resolved.

Consider Michelle and Tommy. They found early in their relationship that they virtually always agreed with each other. Both had been in past relationships that were much rockier, so they were delighted to find a relationship that was almost conflict free. They prided themselves on their widespread agreement and told their friends they doubted there was a couple anywhere who were more compatible. They became serious and got engaged. It was after the engagement that the problems started. As the conversations became more serious—about when to have children, about career aspirations, about where they wanted to live—Michelle found herself less frequently in agreement with Tommy. But she was reluctant to disagree because they so prided themselves on agreeing about practically everything. So she found herself orally agreeing with Tommy even when she felt otherwise. As she found herself agreeing to things that displeased her, she became less satisfied with the relationship. Eventually the relationship faltered and the couple broke up. The couple's need to be agreeable toward each other masked disagreements and negotiations that they needed to have. Their similarity in agreeableness proved, in the end, to be disagreeable. Obviously, there will be other cases where similarity in agreeableness facilitates a couple's relationship. The point here is that similarity can be good or it can be bad.

Conscientiousness is also associated with relationship satisfaction (Botwin, Buss, & Shackelford, 1997; Engel, Olson, &

Patrick, 2002; Karney & Bradbury, 1995; Kwan, Bond, & Singelis, 1997). But in men conscientiousness can be associated with relationship failure (Newcomb & Bentler, 1981). Why would conscientiousness be associated with both success and failure? On the one hand, people who are conscientious are more likely to pay attention to the details of a relationship in a way that leads to greater success—such as remembering important occasions, making sure to pay attention to the needs of the other person, and attending to money matters that, if ignored, could lead to financial problems and marital strife. On the other hand, people who are highly conscientious may set standards for each other, and for themselves, that are hard to meet. They may expect more from the other than that person is able or willing to give, and may find themselves dissatisfied if their high expectations are not met.

Ron and Liz are complementary on conscientiousness. Sometimes this complementarity helps them. Liz needs someone who is conscientious to help her make sure she gets done what she needs to do—both in her work and in her personal life. She values Ron highly for his conscientious nature. At the same time, Ron knows that he can be conscientious to a fault, and he enjoys being with someone who is not nearly as much of a perfectionist as he is. But their complementarity also has its costs. When Ron finds things out of place, he instinctively puts them back to their proper state. Liz almost never puts things back where they belong. Ron is becoming irritated because he seems to be the one who is always putting things away. He is beginning to feel that he is in a relationship with a child who will not put away her toys. He has talked to Liz about the problem several times, and she has pledged to put things away—and she does, for a few days. Then she reverts to her old form and lets things get out of order, frustrating Ron even more. Ron thus finds their complementarity, at times, to be a source of frustration, sticking him with the task of creating order for things that he feels are Liz's responsibility. For this couple, complementarity both helps and hurts the relationship. As this couple illustrates, there is no straightforward correspondence between complementarity and relationship success.

Extraversion as well is associated, overall, with satisfaction in relationships (Bentler & Newcomb, 1978; Kelly & Conley, 1987), but there also are signs that it may be associated with lower satisfaction among men (Bentler & Newcomb, 1978). In other words, being an extravert, like conscientiousness, can be a mixed blessing. On the one hand, two people who are extraverted are more likely to reach out to each other and to seek out company, including each other's. On the other hand, someone who is highly extraverted may form relationships outside the couple that constitute a risk factor for marital infidelity.

David and Beth are both extraverted, David much more so than Beth. David seems to have a need to be with other people in order to remain happy. Beth likes to be with other people but also likes some alone time. She is starting to feel that she needs more space than David seems willing to give her. But there is a more serious problem. David and Beth work in the same office. They both communicate with others, but David is more forward with other women than Beth is comfortable with. When she confronts David about this, he retorts that he is just a friendly person and that Beth would be a lot happier if she were more like him. In this case, involving two extraverted people, dissimilarity in levels of extraversion causes a problem.

The relationship of neuroticism to relationship success is fairly uniformly negative (Karney & Bradbury, 1995; Newcomb & Bentler, 1981). Neuroticism has been associated with infatuation, which generally is not a predictor of long-term relationship success. People who are moody and unstable generally have greater difficulty in all their relationships, of course, not just their intimate ones.

Brenda and Alex have what by any standard would be called a troubled relationship. Alex is very moody. When he is loving and giving toward Brenda, she finds him to be wonderful. But he may be loving and caring one day, but distant and aloof the next. He acts as though Brenda somehow has treated him wrong, but when she asks if she has done anything to offend him, he shrugs off her question. She is not sure whether she has indeed done something he resents or whether he is just being moody. Brenda really wants to change Alex. She thinks if anyone can bring him happiness, she can. But she cannot break through his neuroticism, which seems to be a problem others in his family have had with him as well. Alex just is one of those people who is difficult, regardless of whom he is with. Alex's neuroticism is a sticking point in the relationship, as it is in many such relationships, where one partner is neurotic and the other partner tries somehow to cure his or her neuroticism.

Openness to experience also has a mixed record. It has been found to be negatively associated with success in relationships (Karney & Bradbury, 1995) and also with decreased longevity of relationships (Shaver & Brennan, 1992). This may be because people who are open to experience are open to other relationships and are more willing to experiment with alternative relationships.

Lea and Jason are both low in openness to experience. They have a fixed routine of working on weekdays and playing tennis and golf on the weekends—tennis on Saturday and golf on Sunday. If they miss any of their weekend activities, they feel cheated. They are not particularly interested in trying new things or in seeking new experiences. When they see their friends travel to exotic places, they congratulate themselves on owning a nice home and living in a fashionable community where they feel perfectly contented. Their lack of eagerness to try new things is precisely what makes them so happy to together.

In general, then, agreeableness, conscientiousness, and extraversion tend to be associated with relationship success, and openness to experience and neuroticism are more likely to be negatively associated with success (White, Hendrick, & Hendrick,

2004). Neuroticism is also negatively associated with success in nonintimate relationships. However, the findings, as the preceding examples show, are mixed. What seems more important than the personality traits per se is how they are utilized in a given relationship. What leads to success in one relationship can lead to failure in another. Probably the most important predictor of relationship success, over and above personality, is the intense desire to make the relationship work, even in the face of environmental and other challenges.

Relationship Challenges: Questions and Answers

ow do you use all the things you have learned in this book to help yourself and others through relationship challenges? This chapter provides some questions and answers so that you can see for yourself.

1. *I have caught my boyfriend cheating on me twice. I suspect there may have been other instances as well. He has promised that, once we are married, he will be completely monogamous. He says that, before we are married, he needs to "sow his wild oats," whatever that means. Should I believe him?*

   One principle in psychology is that the best predictor of future behavior of a given kind is past behavior of the same kind (Ajzen, 2005). It is for this reason that psychologists so

CHAPTER 10

frequently look to past behavior to predict how a person will behave in the future. This is not to say that people cannot change; of course they can. But changing is hard, and permanently changing is even harder, as anyone who has tried to lose weight or to stop smoking can attest. So your boyfriend may believe what he tells you, in the same way that the 90% of people who have lost weight and regained it believed in their vow that their diet would lead to permanent weight loss. Bottom line: If he is unable or unwilling to stop cheating now, don't expect him to change in the future. He may change, but you probably would not want to bet the happiness of your future life on it.

2. *My girlfriend and I used to have a really exciting and passionate relationship. Lately, though, our passion seems to have died down a lot. Is it time to break up?*

Most theories of love predict that, as time goes on, the passion in a relationship will begin to falter. For example, according to the triangular theory of love (Sternberg, 1986), passion is the quickest component of a relationship to develop but also the quickest to die down. It functions much like an addiction. Consider an analogy to drinking coffee. When people start drinking coffee, one cup of regular coffee can give them a big caffeine jolt to help them concentrate and perhaps stay awake. However, over time, they habituate to the effects of the caffeine so that one cup of coffee no longer has the same effect; they may need two or more cups to get the same jolt. It is much the same with passion: People habituate to the stimuli that cause them experience passion, and over time, they feel less of a jolt. The question is thus twofold: First, is there any way to maintain passion? Second, is it worth remaining in a relationship once the passion has cooled down?

With regard to the first question, the best way to maintain passion is to keep generating new kinds of excitement with your partner. Try doing new things together, going to new places together, and breaking whatever old routines you have in favor of new ones. You may not be able to re-create the full passion you felt in the very early days of your relationship, but you may be able to generate enough to keep yourself satisfied. The worst enemy of passion is boredom.

With regard to the second question, ask yourself whether you have in full measure the other two elements in the triangular theory of love, namely, intimacy and commitment. If you are good friends—if you experience warmth, compassion, trust, caring, and good communication—and if you are committed to making the relationship work, then you have the basis for a solid long-term relationship, even if, over time, it evolves toward companionate love. Indeed, if you always need the thrill of the early days of a relationship, you may find yourself flitting from one relationship to the next without ever experiencing any deeper satisfaction. Moreover, even if you find yourself in a committed relationship, you may find it to be of short duration. Thus, if the relationship is going strong except for the waning of passion, try to make it work by accepting that passion tends to decline over time and can be renewed, to some extent, by adding excitement to your life together.

3. *My boyfriend and I have been together for 4 years. We have and always have had a good, strong relationship. The problem is that I'm not getting younger, and every time we talk about a permanent commitment he freezes up. He seems to be reluctant to commit to our relationship. We have talked about it and he says he just is not ready. I'm afraid he'll never be ready. What should I do?*

Many people are commitment-phobic, but it often is hard to tell exactly who is phobic and who is just not ready to make a long-term commitment. It depends partly on your age. The pattern you describe is more worrisome if you are 30 than if you are 20 years of age. The fact that he freezes up when you speak of commitment is not a good sign, as it may indicate a deep underlying level of anxiety. One option is to tell him you are really happy in the relationship but you feel that if he is not prepared to commit by a particular date, then you will need to move on. You might even try setting the date together, if he is willing. In any case you should stick with the date you set, and if he is still unwilling to commit, you should move on, difficult though that may be.

There is one other question you should ask yourself. Is there any reason that he is reluctant to commit other than a phobia? Is the relationship all he wants it to be? If not, you need to know that now and find out whether the two of you can make your relationship into the one he wants. You also may want to ask yourself whether the relationship is all *you* want it to be. R. Sternberg's theory of love as a story (Sternberg, 1998) suggests that people have stories about love that are arranged in a hierarchical fashion. We all tend to be attracted to others who have stories similar to our own. We usually do not know what our stories are; we simply feel either a close connection or a more remote one depending on whether we sense a match. For example, if one partner of a couple has a business story and the other has a fairy-tale story, the relationship is going to be challenged, no matter how similar the two individuals are in other respects. One person will be looking for a business partner, the other for a prince or princess. Sternberg's book actually has quizzes a couple can take to determine their stories and whether they match. One thing you should ask yourselves before you commit is whether you have matching stories—whether you are looking for the same things in a loving relationship. If not, then committing to one another may be a mistake, regardless of how similar your values may otherwise be. A mismatch of stories is not as obvious as disagreement over political beliefs, the desire to have children, or religious affiliation, but it can be just as challenging to a relationship.

4. *I am now with a guy who recently broke up with his one-time fiancée. We have a very good relationship and really care about each other. He tells me that I give him everything his ex-fiancée hadn't. For example, the two of them basically stopped making love 3 years ago. The one thing that worries me is how much he talks about his failed relationship. Whenever I try to change the topic, the conversation somehow goes back to his old relationship and how it blew up. How can I get him to move on?*

When people stop drinking coffee or smoking, or taking illegal drugs, for that matter, they typically undergo withdrawal symptoms. The more serious the habit, the longer the withdrawal period lasts. It is not uncommon for people disengaging from intimate relationships to experience withdrawal symptoms. Your partner seems to be in that stage, especially given that he recently broke up with his fiancée. The upside for purposes of your relationship is that you snared him before someone else did. If he is a good catch, you have done well for yourself. The downside in terms of your relationship is that you are facing three fairly substantial risks.

First, it is not uncommon for two people who break up to get back together again. It may be that your new boyfriend not only has failed to move beyond his old relationship, but will discover through this relationship with you that, whatever the problems he experienced in that relationship, he still desires to go back to it. Or his former fiancée may pressure him to return to her. Your first risk, therefore, is that you will lose the guy to his former fiancée.

Second, when people end serious relationships, they often go through a period in which they are just not ready to enter a new relationship. In effect, they have to detach themselves from the last relationship before they can attach themselves to a new one. In terms of the triangular theory of love (Sternberg, 1986), if they are still experiencing withdrawal symptoms, they are very susceptible to being drawn back to their old habit. The fact that your boyfriend seems unable to stop talking about his last relationship, even when you try to get him to stop, suggests he is not over it and may just need a break from serious relationships.

Third, you need to ensure that you are not in a relationship on the rebound. When a person finishes a relationship, he or she sometimes looks for someone who, at least at a superficial level, is everything the first partner was not. At a deeper level, the new and old partners may actually be much more similar than the rebounder realizes. Such relationships on the rebound have a rather poor prognosis. If such a relationship ends up becoming serious, there is a good chance it will end badly. More often, however, it ends when the individual on the rebound is truly ready to start a new relationship and wants to be with someone who does not serve as a reminder of the old relationship.

So, caveat emptor: Buyer beware! The kind of relationship you describe is fraught with risk, but if you are confident it is what you want, by all means try to make it work.

5. *My relationship with my girlfriend would be perfect were she not so jealous. She seems to be constantly monitoring my behavior and looking for signs that I am romantically interested in someone else. She seems to exaggerate the importance of any positive reaction I show to another woman, even if I'm just being friendly. I really love her and would like to "cure" her of her jealousy. How do I do that?*

You don't. People who tend to be jealous often are dispositionally inclined to be that way and it is extremely difficult and sometimes just not possible to change them. Often, they adopt what Lee (1977) has referred to as a manic love style—moving from one extreme to the other. Manic lovers can feel extremely passionate and close to a partner one day, and extremely alienated the next. They tend to be possessive and jealous. So "How do I do that?" is probably not the right question. Here are three questions to ask instead.

First, if your partner were to remain a jealous person, is this something you could live with? If the answer is no, you should minimize your losses. The chances of her changing into a person who is secure are not great. Jealous people are especially likely to have what Shaver, Hazan, and Bradshaw (1988) refer to as an anxious/ambivalent attachment style. They come very close at one point, and then pull away. Love relationships with them are typically somewhat tumultuous.

Second, will she stay with you? If she is jealous now, her jealousy may actually get worse as your level of commitment increases and the cost of a breakup therefore becomes much greater. At some point, she may toss you aside if she decides you are just too unreliable to be a satisfactory partner. Of course, she may display the same behavior in subsequent relationships as well.

Third, is there anything you are doing that may be a legitimate cause of her jealousy? Up to now, we have been assuming the problem is with her. But is it? Is it possible that you have a roving eye and are seeking to project the blame for your own problematical behavior onto her? Only you can provide an honest answer to that question. Are you, to any extent, a cause of your current woes?

6. *When we first met, my boyfriend and I seemed to be able to talk about anything. We had deep conversations and nothing seemed to be out of bounds for discussion. As time has gone on, however, our conversations have become more and more superficial. I'm not sure what's happened, but we seem to have settled into a somewhat dull routine. I actually think we are less intimate than we were during the early months of our relationship. Does this mean our relationship is failing?*

The situation you describe is actually quite common in relationships and in fact is predicted by the triangular theory of love (Sternberg, 1986). When you first meet, intimacy has some risks; for example, if your partner is unreliable, he may spill your secrets to others. But there is one kind of risk you do not have to face, and it involves secrets that you are keeping about your own relationship. It is easy to talk about all the things you did wrong in your last relationship, but much harder to talk about the things you have done wrong in the current relationship.

One reason this apparent decrease in intimacy occurs is that life intervenes. When you first meet, the relationship often takes precedence over everything else. But you can't keep the rest of your life on hold forever, and often, as time goes on, you find yourself presented with more and more other things to deal with. It is for this reason that relationships genuinely require hard work. They do not maintain themselves. You have to make an effort to maintain them, and especially to maintain the flow of communication within them. Don't expect it just to happen on its own.

It sometimes is hard to know whether you are experiencing a lull in communication due to life intervening or whether the relationship is genuinely going downhill. The best way to find out may be to have a hiatus, as happens when you and your partner are separated for a while. If, when you are separated, you confirm the adage that "absence makes the heart grow fonder," your relationship probably is doing well. If, on the other hand, you find there is more truth in "out of sight, out of mind," you may be in trouble.

Vaughn (1990) performed a brilliant analysis of breakups and concluded that they usually begin with a secret. One partner has a secret that he or she does not share with the other partner. As time goes on, the secret becomes harder to conceal, or other secrets started to accumulate. Once one starts keeping secrets, where does one stop? So a question to ask yourself is whether a drop in communication is due to your simply being too busy, or whether it is due, even in part, to increased reluctance to talk about important things. If the latter is the case, unless you can bring yourself to talk about those things, the relationship might be in trouble.

7. *I'm not sure whether my girlfriend is in love with me or with an image of me. I have been lucky in having a lot of success in my life. I graduated second in my class in college. Now I'm in medical school and I expect to be a surgeon. Whenever we talk about our future, I have the feeling that she is in love with the idea of being married to a surgeon. How do I find out whether she is in love with me or just her image of me and the life we will have together?*

According to the theory of love as a story, all we ever know of another person is filtered through our stories of that other. So in one sense, you can never know for sure if another person is in love with who you truly are because another person can never know who you truly are. Indeed, Goffman (1990) argues that there is no one "real self." Rather, one is the roles one plays. So here are questions you might ask yourself: Is the life your girlfriend envisions a life with which you will be happy? If not, have you discussed with her the kind of life you would like? If not, why not? Finally, are you sure your image of her is correct?

Sternberg and Barnes (1985) found that there is only a weak relation between what we think a romantic partner feels about us and what the partner actually feels. So it is not uncommon for people to find disparities in their images of each other. The important thing to ask is whether you both have the same image of a life together and, if not, whether there is at least enough similarity to make a life together viable.

These are some of the many questions that psychological research can help you answer about romantic relationships. The number of questions is unlimited. And so is the capacity of psychology to help you understand love and its manifestations in close relationships. Good luck in yours!

References

Acevedo, B., Arthur, A., Fisher, H. E., & Brown, L. L. (2012). Neural correlates of long-term intense romantic love. *Scan, 7,* 145–159.

Ackerman, J. M., Ledlow, S. E., & Kenrick, D. T. (2003). *Friends are family, friends are strangers: Social cognition in social relationships.* Paper presented at the annual meeting of the Society for Personality and Social Psychology, Austin, TX.

Adler, N. L., Hendrick, S. S., & Hendrick, C. (1986). Male sexual preference and attitudes toward love and sexuality. *Journal of Sex Education and Therapy, 12*(2), 27–30.

Ainsworth, M. D. S. (1989). Attachments beyond infancy. *American Psychologist, 44,* 709–716.

Algoe, S. B., Gable, S. L., & Maisel, N. C. (2010). It's the little things: Everyday gratitude as a booster shot for romantic relationships. *Personal Relationships, 17,* 217–233.

Amato, P. R., Booth, A., Johnson, D. R., & Rogers, S. J. (2007). *Alone together: How marriage in America is changing.* Cambridge, MA: Harvard University Press.

Amato, P. R., & Previti, D. (2003). People's reasons for divorcing: Gender, social class, the life course, and adjustment. *Journal of Family Issues, 24*(5), 602–626.

Amichai-Hamburger, Y., Kingsbury, M., & Schneider, B. H. (2013). Friendship: An old concept with new meaning? *Computers in Human Behavior, 29,* 33–39.

Aries, P. (1962). *Centuries of childhood: A social history of family life.* New York, NY: Vintage.

Aron, A., Dutton, D. G., Aron, E. N., & Iverson, A. (1989). Experiences of falling in love. *Journal of Social and Personal Relationships, 6,* 243–257.

Aronson, E., & Linder, D. (1965). Gain and loss of esteem as determinants of interpersonal attractiveness. *Journal of Experimental Social Psychology, 1,* 156–172.

Asendorpf, J. B., Penke, L., & Back, M. D. (2011). From dating to mating and relating: Predictors of initial and long-term outcomes of speed-dating in a community sample. *European Journal of Personality, 25,* 16–30.

Azjen, I. (2005). *Attitudes, personality, and behavior* (2nd ed.). Maidenhead, Berkshire, UK: Open University Press.

Back, M. D., Schmukle, S. C., & Egloff, B. (2008). Becoming friends by chance. *Psychological Science, 19,* 439–440.

Backman, C. W., & Secord, P. F. (1959). The effect of perceived liking on interpersonal attraction. *Human Relations, 12,* 379–384.

Bartels, A., & Zeki, S. (2000). The neural basis of romantic love. *NeuroReport, 11,* 3829–3834.

Bartels, A., & Zeki, S. (2004). The neural correlates of maternal and romantic love. *NeuroImage, 21,* 1155–1166.

Bartholomew, K., & Horowitz, L. M. (1991). Attachment styles among young adults: A test of a four-category model. *Journal of Personality and Social Psychology, 61,* 226–244.

Beauregard, M., Levesque, J., & Bourgouin, P. (2001). Neural correlates of conscious self-regulation of emotion. *Journal of Neuroscience, 21*(18), RC165.

Belsky, J., Steinberg, L., & Draper, P. (1991). Childhood experience, interpersonal development, and reproductive strategy: An evolutionary theory of socialization. *Child Development, 62,* 647–670.

Bentler, P. M., & Newcomb, M. D. (1978). Longitudinal study of marital success and failure. *Journal of Consulting and Clinical Psychology, 46,* 1053–1070.

Berscheid, E. (1985). Interpersonal attraction. In G. Lindzey & E. Aronson (Eds.), *The handbook of social psychology* (3rd ed., Vol. 2, pp. 413–484). New York, NY: Random House.

Berscheid, E. (2006a). Searching for the meaning of "love." In R. J. Sternberg & K. Weis (Eds.), *The new psychology of love* (pp. 171–183). New Haven, CT: Yale University Press.

Berscheid, E. (2006b). Seasons of the heart. In M. Mikulincer & G. Goodwin (Eds.), *Dynamics of love: Attachment, caregiving, and sex* (pp. 404–422). New York, NY: Guilford Press.

Berscheid, E. (2010). Love in the fourth dimension. *Annual Review of Psychology, 61,* 1–25.

Berscheid, E., & Regan, P. (2005). *The psychology of interpersonal relationships.* New York, NY: Prentice Hall.

Bertrand, M., & Mullainathan, S. (2004). Are Emily and Greg more employable than Lakisha and Jamal? A field experiment on labor market discrimination. *American Economic Review, 94,* 991–1013.

Boothroyd, L. G., Jones, B. C., Burt, D. M., DeBruine, L. M., & Perret, D. I. (2008). Facial correlates of sociosexuality. *Evolution and Human Behavior, 29,* 211–218.

Botwin, M. D., Buss, D. M., & Shackelford, T. K. (1997). Personality and mate preferences: Five factors in mate selection and marital satisfaction. *Journal of Personality, 66,* 107–136.

Bowlby, J. (1969/1982). *Attachment and loss: Vol. 1. Attachment* (2nd ed.). New York, NY: Basic Books.

Bowlby, J. (1980). *Attachment and loss: Vol. 3. Sadness and depression.* New York, NY: Basic Books.

Brand, R. J., Bonatsos, A., D'Orazio, R., & DeShong, H. (2012). What is beautiful is good even online: Correlations between photo attractiveness and text attractiveness in men's online dating profiles. *Computers in Human Behavior, 28,* 166–170.

Brown, S. L., Bulanda, J. R., & Lee, G. R. (2012). Transitions into and out of cohabitation in later life. *Journal of Marriage and the Family, 74,* 774–793.

Brown, S. L., Lin, I.-F., & Payne, K. K. (2012). *Age variation in the divorce rate, 1990–2010* (FP-12-05). National Center for Family & Marriage Research. Retrieved from http://ncfmr.bgsu.edu/pdf/family_profiles/file108695.pdf

Bumpass, L., & Lu, H.-H. (2000). frends in cohabitation and implications for children's family contexts in the United States. *Population Studies 54*(1), 29–41.

Buss, D. M. (2006). The evolution of love. In R. J. Sternberg & K. Weis (Eds.), *The new psychology of love* (pp. 65–86). New Haven, CT: Yale University Press.

Buston, P. M., & Emlen, S. T. (2003). Cognitive processes underlying human mate choice: The relationship between self-perception and mate preferences in Western society. *Proceedings of the National Academy of Sciences of the United States of America, 100,* 8805–8810.

Byrne, D., & Clore, G. L. (1970). A reinforcement model of evaluative processes. *Personality: An International Journal, 1*, 103–128.

Byrne, D., & Griffitt, W. (1973). Interpersonal attraction. *Annual Review of Psychology, 17*, 316–336.

Byrne, D., & Nelson, D. (1965). Attraction as a linear function of proportion of positive reinforcements. *Journal of Personality and Social Psychology, 1*, 659–663.

Canary, D. J., & Stafford, L. (1992). Relational maintenance strategies and equity in marriage. *Communication Monographs, 59*, 243–265.

Chisholm, J. S. (1999). Steps to an evolutionary ecology of the mind. In A. L. Hinton (Ed.), *Biocultural approaches to the emotions* (pp. 117–149). Cambridge, UK: Cambridge University Press.

Clark, M. L., & Drewry, D. L. (1985). Similarity and reciprocity in the friendships of elementary school children. *Child Study Journal, 15*(4), 251–264.

Clark, M. S., & Finkel, E. J. (2005). Willingness to express emotion: The impact of relationship type, communal orientation and their interaction. *Personality Relationships, 12*, 169–180.

Clark, M. S., & Mills, J. R. (2012). A theory of communal (and exchange) relationships. In A. W. Kruglanski & E. T. Higgins (Eds.), *Handbook of theories of social psychology* (Vol. 2, pp. 232–250). Thousand Oaks, CA: Sage.

Clark, M. S., & Monin, J. K. (2006). Giving and receiving communal responsiveness as love. In R. J. Sternberg & K. Weis (Eds.), *The new psychology of love* (pp. 200–221). New Haven, CT: Yale University Press.

Clore, G. L., & Byrne, D. (1974). A reinforcement-affect model of attraction. In T. L. Huston (Ed.), *Foundations of interpersonal attraction* (pp. 143–170). New York, NY: Academic Press.

Cohan, C. L., & Cole, S. (2002). Life course transitions and natural disaster: Marriage, birth, and divorce following Hurricane Hugo. *Journal of Family Psychology, 16*, 14–25.

Cohan, C. L., & Kleinbaum, S. (2002). Toward a greater understanding of the cohabitation effect: Premarital cohabitation and marital communication. *Journal of Marriage and the Family, 64*, 180–192.

Cohan, C. L., & Schoen, R. (2009). Divorce following the September 11 terrorist attacks. *Journal of Social and Personal Relationships, 26*, 512–531.

Cohen, G. L., & Garcia, J. (2008). Identity, belonging, and achievement: A model, interventions, implications. *Current Directions in Psychological Science, 17*, 365–369.

Collins, N. L., & Read, S. J. (1990). Adult attachment, working models, and relationship quality in dating couples. *Journal of Personality and Social Psychology, 58*, 644–663.

Conley, T. D., Roesch, S. C., Peplau, L. A., & Gold, M. S. (2009). A test of positive illusions versus shared reality models of relationship satisfaction among gay, lesbian, and heterosexual couples. *Journal of Applied Social Psychology, 39*, 1417–1431.

Costa, P. T., Jr., & McCrae, R. R. (1992). *Revised NEO Personality Inventory (NEO-PI-R) and NEO Five-Factor Inventory (NEO-FFI) manual.* Odessa, FL: Psychological Assessment Resources.

Couch, D., Liamputtong, P., & Pitts, M. (2012). What are the real and perceived risks and dangers of online dating? Perspectives from online daters. *Health, Risk, and Society, 14*(7–8), 679–714.

Cunningham, M., & Thornton, A. (2005). The influences of parents' and offsprings' experience with cohabitation, marriage, and divorce on attitudes toward divorce in young adulthood. *Journal of Divorce and Remarriage, 44*, 119–144.

Cunningham, M. R., Barbee, A. P., & Pike, C. L. (1990). What do women want? Facialmetric assessment of multiple motives in the perception of male facial physical attractiveness. *Journal of Personality and Social Psychology, 59*, 61–72.

Cunningham, M. R., Roberts, A. R., Barbee, A. P., Druen, P. B., & Wu, C. (1995). "Their ideas of beauty are, on the whole, the same as ours": Consistency and variability in the cross-cultural perception of female physical attractiveness. *Journal of Personality and Social Psychology, 68*, 261–279.

Cuperman, R., & Ickes, W. (2009). Big five predictors of behavior and perceptions in initial dyadic interactions: Personality similarity helps extraverts and introverts but hurts "disagreeables." *Journal of Personality and Social Psychology, 97*, 667–684.

deMunck, V. C., Korotayev, A., deMunck, J., & Khaltourina, D. (2011). Cross-cultural analysis of models of romantic love among U.S. residents, Russians, and Lithuanians. *Cross-Cultural Research, 45*(2), 128–154.

DeWall, C. N., & Pond, R. S. (2011). Loneliness and smoking: The costs of the desire to reconnect. *Self and Identity, 10*, 375–385.

Dion, K. K., Berscheid, E., & Walster, E. (1972). What is beautiful is what is good. *Journal of Personality and Social Psychology, 24*, 285–290.

Dion, K. K., & Dion, K. L. (1991). Psychological individualism and romantic love. *Journal of Social Behavior and Personality, 6*, 17–33.

Dion, K. K., & Dion, K. L. (1993). Individualistic and collectivistic perspectives on gender and the cultural context of love and intimacy. *Journal of Social Issues, 49*, 53–69.

Dion, K. K. & Dion, K. L. (2006). Individualism, collectivism, and the psychology of love. In R. J. Sternberg & K. Weis (Eds.), *The new psychology of love* (pp. 298–312). New Haven, CT: Yale University Press.

Dion, K. L., & Dion, K. K. (1993). Gender and ethnocultural comparisons in styles of love. *Psychology of Women Quarterly, 17*, 463–473.

Dion, K. L., & Dion, K. K. (2005). Culture and relationships: The downside of self-contained individualism. In R. M. Sorrentino, D. Cohen, J. M. Olson, & M. Zanna (Eds.), *Culture and social behavior: The Ontario Symposium* (Vol. 10, pp. 77–94). Mahwah, NJ: Erlbaum.

Doherty, R. W., Hatfield, E., Thompson, K., & Choo, P. (1994). Cultural and ethnic influences on love and attachment. *Personal Relationships, 1*, 391–398.

Dunn, E. W., Wilson, T. D., & Gilbert, D. T. (2003). Location, location, location: The misprediction of satisfaction in housing lotteries. *Personality and Social Psychology Bulletin, 29*, 1421–1432.

Eagly, A. H., Ashmore, R. D., Makhijani, M. G., & Longo, L. C. (1991). What is beautiful is good, but. . . : A meta-analytic review of research on the physical attractiveness stereotype. *Psychological Bulletin, 110*, 109–128.

Edenfield, J. L., Adams, K. S., & Briihl, D. S. (2012). Relationship maintenance strategy use by romantic attachment style. *North American Journal of Psychology, 14*(1), 149–162.

eHarmony.com. (2013, February 25). Retrieved from http://www.eharmony.com

Elliot, A. J., Kayser, D. N., Greitemeyer, T., Lichtenfeld, S., Gramzow, R. H., Maier, M. A., & Liu, H. (2010). Red, rank, and romance in women viewing men. *Journal of Experimental Psychology, 139*(3), 399–417.

Engel, G., Olson, K. R., & Patrick, C. (2002). The personality of love: Fundamental motives and traits related to components of love. *Personality and Individual Differences, 32,* 839–853.

Fehr, B. (1995). *Friendship processes.* Thousand Oaks, CA: Sage.

Festinger, L., Schachter, S., & Back, K. (1950). *Social pressures in informal groups: A study of human factors in housing.* Stanford, CA: Stanford University Press.

Fink, B., Neave, N., Manning, J. T., & Grammer, K. (2006). Facial symmetry and judgments of attractiveness, health, and personality. *Personality and Individual Differences, 41,* 491–499.

Finkel, E. J., Eastwick, P. W., Karney, B. R., Reis, H. R., & Sprecher, S. (2012). Online dating: A critical analysis from the perspective of psychological science. *Psychological Science in the Public Interest, 13*(1), 3–66.

Fiore, A. T., Taylor, L. S., Mendelsohn, G. A., & Hearst, M. (2008). Assessing attractiveness in online dating profiles. In *Proceedings of the 26th annual SIGCHI conference on Computer-Human Interaction* (pp. 797–806). New York, NY: ACM Press.

Fisher, H. (1998). Lust, attraction, and attachment in mammalian reproduction. *Human Nature, 9*(1), 23–52.

Fisher, H. (2004). *Why we love: The nature and chemistry of romantic love.* New York, NY: Henry Holt.

Fisher, H. (2006). The drive to love: The neural mechanism for mate selection. In R. J. Sternberg & K. Weis (Eds.), *The new psychology of love* (pp. 87–115). New Haven, CT: Yale University Press.

Fisher, H., Aron, A., Mashek, D., Strong, G., Li, H., & Brown, L. L. (2003). *Early stage intense romantic love activates cortical-basal-ganglia reward/motivation, emotion and attention systems: An fMRI study of a dynamic network that varies with relationship length, passion intensity and gender.* Poster presented at the Annual Meeting of the Society for Neuroscience, New Orleans, November 11.

Fonteille, V., & Stoleru, S. (2011). The cerebral correlates of sexual desire: Functional neuroimaging approach. *Sexologies, 20,* 142–148.

Fraley, R. C., Waller, N. G., & Brennan, K. A. (2000). An item response theory analysis of self-report measures of adult attachment. *Journal of Personality and Social Psychology, 78,* 350–365.

Freud, S. (1955). Certain neurotic mechanisms in jealousy, paranoia, and homosexuality. In S. Freud (Ed.), *Collected papers* (Vol. 2, pp. 235, 240, 323). London: Hogarth Press. (Original work published 1922)

Frieze, I. H., Olson, J. E., & Russell, J. (1991). Attractiveness and income for men and women in management. *Journal of Applied Social Psychology, 21*(13), 1039–1057.

Frost, J. H., Chance, Z., Norton, M. I., & Ariely, D. (2008). People are experience goods: Improving online dating with virtual dates. *Journal of Interactive Marketing, 22*, 51–61.

Gallant, S., Williams, L., Fisher, M., & Cox, A. (2011). Mating strategies and self-presentation in online personal advertisement photographs. *Journal of Social, Evolutionary, and Cultural Psychology, 5*(1), 106–121.

Gangestad, S. W., & Buss, D. M. (1993). Pathogen prevalence and human mate preferences. *Ethology and Sociobiology, 14*, 89–96.

Gangestad, S. W., & Thornhill, R. (1997). The evolutionary psychology of extrapair sex: The role of fluctuating asymmetry. *Evolution and Human Behavior, 18*, 69–88.

Gangestad, S. W., Thornhill, R., & Garver-Apgar, C. E. (2010). Fertility in the cycle predicts women's interest in sexual opportunism. *Evolution and Human Behavior, 31*, 400–411.

Gao, G. (2001). Intimacy, passion and commitment in Chinese and U.S. American romantic relationships. *International Journal of Intercultural Relations, 25*, 329–342.

Gaunt, R. (2006). Couple similarity and marital satisfaction: Are similar spouses happier? *Journal of Personality, 74*(5), 1401–1420.

Geary, D. C. (1998). *Male, female: The evolution of human sex differences.* Washington, DC: American Psychological Association.

Gebauer, J. E., Leary, M. R., & Neberich, W. (2012). Unfortunate first names: Effects of name-based relational devaluation and interpersonal neglect. *Social Psychological and Personality Science, e*(5), 590–596.

GenePartner.com. (2013, February 25). Retrieved from http://www.genepartner.com

Gibbons, A. (2004). Tracking the evolutionary history of a "warrior" gene. *Science, 304*, 818–819.

Gibbs, J. L., Ellison, N. B., & Lai, C. (2011). Reduction strategies and self-disclosure in online dating: First comes love, then comes Google: An investigation of uncertainty. *Communication Research, 38*(1), 70–100.

Gigy, L., & Kelly, J. B. (1992). Reasons for divorce: Perspectives of divorcing men and women. *Journal of Divorce & Remarriage, 18*, 169–188.

Gingrich, B., Liu, Y., Cascio, C., Wang, Z., & Insel, T. R. (2000). Dopamine D2 receptors in the nucleus accumbens are important for social attachment in female prairie voles (microtus ochrogaster). *Behavioral Neuroscience, 114*(1), 173–183.

Gladue, B. A., & Delaney, H. (1990). Gender differences in perception of attractiveness of men and women in bars. *Personality and Social Psychology Bulletin, 16*, 378–391.

Glasser, C. L., Robnett, B., & Feliciano, C. (2009). Internet daters' body type preferences: Race-ethnic and gender differences. *Sex Roles, 61*(1–2), 14–33.

Goel, S., Mason, W., & Watts, D. J. (2010). Real and perceived attitude agreement in social networks. *Journal of Personality and Social Psychology, 99*, 611–621.

Goffman, E. (1990). *The presentation of self in everyday life.* London: Penguin.

Goldberg, L. R. (1993). The structure of phenotypic personality traits. *American Psychologist, 48*(1), 26–34.

Gonzaga, G. C., Carter, S., & Buckwalter, G. J. (2010). Assortative mating, convergence, and satisfaction in married couples. *Personal Relationships, 17*, 634–644.

Gonzales, J. E., & Luevano, V. X. (2011). *Forget the little black dress: Fertility, women's use of red, sexual desire, and men's mating-effort.* Retrieved from http://psychology.ucdavis.edu/images/FCK_Uploads/research/bb/file/JEG_EstrusRed_SPSP2011.pdf

Goodwin, P. Y., Mosher, W. D., & Chandra, A. (2010). Marriage and cohabitation in the United States: A statistical portrait based on Cycle 6 (2002) of the National Survey of Family Growth. *Vital and Health Statistics, 23*(28). Retrieved from http://www.cdc.gov/nchs/data/series/sr_23/sr23_028.pdf

Gordon, A. M., Impett, E. A., Kogan, A., Oveis, C., & Keltner, D. (2012). To have and to hold: Gratitude promotes relationship maintenance in intimate bonds. *Journal of Personality and Social Psychology, 103*(2), 257–274.

Gordon, C. L., Arnette, R. A. M., & Smith, R. E. (2011). Have you thanked your spouse today? Felt and expressed gratitude among married couples. *Personality and Individual Differences, 50*, 339–343.

Grote, N. K., & Clark, M. S. (2001). Perceiving unfairness in the family: Cause or consequence of marital distress? *Journal of Personality and Social Psychology, 80*, 281–293.

Grote, N. K., & Frieze, L. H. (1994). The measurement of friendship-based love in intimate relationships. *Personal Relationships, 1*, 275–300.

Gueguen, N. (2009). Menstrual cycle phases and female receptivity to a courtship solicitation: An evaluation in a nightclub. *Evolution and Human Behavior, 30*, 351–355.

Hamer, D., Hu, S., Magnuson, V., & Pattatucci, A. M. (1993). A linkage between DNA markers on the X chromosome and male sexual orientation. *Science, 261*, 321–327.

Hamermesh, D. S., & Biddle, J. E. (1994). Beauty and the labor market. *American Economic Review, 84*(5), 1174–1194.

Hammock, G., & Richardson, D. S. (2011). Love attitudes and relationship experience. *Journal of Social Psychology, 151*(5), 608–624.

Hatfield, E. (1988). Passionate and companionate love. In R. J. Sternberg & M. L. Barnes (Eds.), *The psychology of love*. New Haven, CT: Yale University Press.

Hatfield, E., Pillemer, J. T., O'Brien, M. U., & Le, Y. L. (2008). The endurance of love: Passionate and companionate love in newlywed and long-term marriages. *Interpersona, 2*, 35–64.

Hazan, C., & Shaver, P. R. (1987). Romantic love conceptualized as an attachment process. *Journal of Personality and Social Psychology, 52*, 511–524.

Heider, F. (1958). *The psychology of interpersonal relations*. New York, NY: Wiley.

Hendrick, C., & Hendrick, S. S. (1986). A theory and method of love. *Journal of Personality and Social Psychology, 50*, 392–402.

Hendrick, C., & Hendrick, S. S. (2006). Styles of romantic love. In R. J. Sternberg & K. Weis (Eds.), *The new psychology of love* (pp. 149–170). New Haven, CT: Yale University Press.

Hendrick, C., Hendrick, S. S., & Dicke, A. (1998). The Love Attitudes Scale: Short form. *Journal of Social and Personal Relationships, 15*, 137–142.

Hendrick, S. S., & Hendrick, C. (1987a). Love and sex attitudes: A close relationship. In W. H. Jones & D. Perlman (Eds.), *Advances in personal relationships* (Vol. 1, pp. 141–169). Greenwich, CT: JAI Press.

Hendrick, S. S., & Hendrick, C. (1987b). Love and sex attitudes and religious beliefs. *Journal of Social and Clinical Psychology, 5*, 391–398.

Herbst, K. C., Gaertner, L., & Insko, C. A. (2003). My head says yes but my heart says no: Cognitive and affective attraction as a function of similarity to the ideal self. *Journal of Personality and Social Psychology, 84*, 1206–1219.

Hetherington, E. M. (2003). Intimate pathways: Changing patterns in close personal relationships across time. *Family Relations, 52*, 318–331.

Hetsroni, A. (2012). Associations between television viewing and love styles: An interpretation using cultivation theory. *Psychological Reports, 110*(1), 35–50.

Hitsch, G. J., Hortaçsu, A., & Ariely, D. (2010a). Matching and sorting in online dating. *American Economic Review, 100*(1), 130–163.

Hitsch, G. J., Hortaçsu, A., & Ariely, D. (2010b). What makes you click? Mate preferences in online dating. *Quantitative Marketing and Economics, 8*, 393–427.

Hohmann-Marriott, B. E. (2006). Shared beliefs and the union stability of married and cohabiting couples. *Journal of Marriage and Family, 68*, 1015–1028.

Homans, G. C. (1974). *Social behavior: Its elementary forms* (Rev. ed.). New York, NY: Harcourt Brace Jovanovich.

Hope, D. (1987). The healing paradox of forgiveness. *Psychotherapy, 24*, 240–244.

Hughes, S. M., & Gallup, G. G., Jr. (2003). Sex differences in morphological predictors of sexual behavior: Shoulder to hip and waist to hip ratios. *Evolution and Human Behavior, 24*, 173–178.

Imamoglu, E. O. (2004). Family. Modern Islamic discourses: Turkey and the Caucasus. In S. Joseph (Ed.), *Encyclopedia of women and Islamic cultures, Vol. 2: Family, law, and politics* (pp. 165–166). Leiden, Netherlands: Brill.

Ingersoll-Dayton, B., Campbell, R., Kurokawa, Y., & Saito, M. (1996). Separateness and togetherness: Interdependence over the life course in Japanese and American marriages. *Journal of Social and Personal Relationships, 3*(13), 385–398.

Inman-Amos, J., Hendrick, S. S., & Hendrick, C. (1994). Love attitudes: Similarities between parents and between parents and children. *Family Relations, 43*, 456–461.

Iyengar, S. S., & Lepper, M. R. (2000). When choice is demotivating: Can one desire too much of a good thing? *Journal of Personality and Social Psychology, 79*, 995–1006.

Jankowiak, W. R., & Fischer, E. F. (1992). A cross-cultural perspective on romantic love. *Ethology, 31*, 149–155.

Jones, D. (1995). Sexual selection, physical attractiveness, and facial neotony: Cross-cultural evidence and implications. *Current Anthropology, 36*, 723–748.

Jones, J. T., Pelham, B. W., Carvallo, M., & Mirenberg, M. C. (2004). How do I love thee? Let me count the Js: Implicit egotism and interpersonal attraction. *Journal of Personality and Social Psychology, 87*, 665–683.

Jose, A., O'Leary, D. K., & Moyer, A. (2010). Does premarital cohabitation predict subsequent marital stability and marital quality? A meta-analysis. *Journal of Marriage and the Family, 72*, 105–116.

Kalist, D. E., & Lee, D. Y. (2009). First names and crime: Does unpopularity spell trouble? *Social Science Quarterly, 90*(1), 39–49.

Karney, B. R., & Bradbury, T. N. (1995). The longitudinal course of marital quality and stability: A review of theory, method, and research. *Psychological Bulletin, 188*, 3–34.

Kelley, D. L. (1998). The communication of forgiveness. *Communication Studies, 49*, 255–271.

Kelley, H. H., Berscheid, E., Christensen, A., Harvey, J. H., Huston, T. L., Levinger, G., McClintock, E., Peplay, L. A., & Peterson, D. R. (2002). *Close relationships.* Clinton Corners, NY: Percheron.

Kelly, E. L., & Conley, J. J. (1987). Personality and compatibility: A prospective analysis of marital stability and marital satisfaction. *Journal of Personality and Social Psychology, 52*, 27–40.

Kendall, T. (2011). The relationship between Internet access and divorce rate. *Journal of Family and Economic Issues, 32*(3), 449–460.

Kendler, K. S., Thornton, L. M., Gilman, S. E., & Kessler, R. C. (2000). Sexual orientation in a U.S. national sample of twin and nontwin sibling pairs. *American Journal of Psychiatry, 157*, 1843–1846.

Kenrick, D. T. (2006). A dynamical evolutionary view of love. In R. J. Sternberg & K. Weis (Eds.), *The new psychology of love* (pp. 15–34). New Haven, CT: Yale University Press.

Kerckhoff, A. C., & Davis, K. (1972). Value consensus and need complementarity in mate selection. *American Sociological Review, 27*, 295–303.

Kirkpatrick, L. A. (1998). Evolution, pair-bonding, and reproductive strategies: A reconceptualization of adult attachment. In J. A. Simpson & W. S. Rholes (Eds.), *Attachment theory and close relationships* (pp. 353–393). New York, NY: Guilford Press.

Kline, G. H., Stanley, S. M., Markman, H. J., Olmos-Gallo, P. A., St. Peters, M., Whitton, S. W., & Prado, L. M. (2004). Timing is everything: Pre-engagement cohabitation and increased risk for poor marital outcomes. *Journal of Family Psychology, 18*, 311–318.

Klohnen, E. C. & Luo, S. (2003). Interpersonal attraction and personality: What is attractive—self similarity, ideal similarity, complementarity, or attachment security? *Journal of Personality and Social Psychology, 85*, 709–722.

Kraus, M. W., & Keltner, D. (2009). Signs of socioeconomic status: A thin-slicing approach. *Psychological Science, 20*, 99–106.

Kruglanski, A. W., & Ajzen, I. (1983). Bias and error in human judgment. *European Journal of Social Psychology, 13*, 1–44.

Kurzban, R., & Weeden, J. (2005). HurryDate: Mate preferences in action. *Evolution and Human Behavior, 26*, 227–244.

Kwan, V. S. Y., Bond, M. H., & Singelis, T. M. (1997). Pancultural explanations for life satisfaction: Adding relationship harmony to self-esteem. *Journal of Personality and Social Psychology, 73*, 1038–1051.

Langlois, J. H., Roggman, L. A., & Musselman, L. (1994). What is average and what is not average about attractive faces? *Psychological Science, 5*, 214–220.

Lassek, W. D., & Gaulin, S. J. C. (2009). Costs and benefits of fat-free muscle mass in men: Relationship to mating success, dietary requirements, and native immunity. *Evolution and Human Behavior, 30*, 322–328.

Le, B., Dove, N. L., Agnew, C. R., Korn, M. S., & Mutso, A. A. (2010). Predicting non-marital romantic relationship dissolution: A meta-analytic synthesis. *Personal Relationships, 17*, 377–390.

Leary, M. R., & Baumeister, R. F. (2000). The nature and function of self-esteem: Sociometer theory. In *Advances in experimental social psychology* (Vol. 32, pp. 1–62). San Diego, CA: Academic Press.

Ledlow, S. E., & Linder, D. E. (2003). *Kinship, familiarity and frame in a simulated social dilemma.* Paper presented at the annual meeting of the Western Psychological Association, Vancouver, BC.

Lee, J. A. (1973). *The colours of love: An exploration of the ways of loving.* Don Mills, Ontario: New Press.

Lee, J. A. (1977). A topology of styles of loving. *Personality and Social Psychology Bulletin, 3*, 173–182.

Lee, J. A. (1988). Love styles. In R. J. Sternberg & M. L. Barnes (Eds.), *The psychology of love* (pp. 38–67). New Haven, CT: Yale University Press.

Levine, R., Sato, S., Hashimoto, T., & Verma, J. (1995). Love and marriage in eleven cultures. *Journal of Cross-Cultural Psychology, 26*, 554–571.

Lichter, D. T., Qian, Z., & Mellott, L. (2006). Marriage or dissolution? Union transitions among poor cohabiting women. *Demography, 43*(2), 223–240.

Lim, M. M., Murphy, A. Z., & Young, L. J. (2004). Ventral striatopallidal oxytocin and vasopressin VIa receptors in the monogamous prairie vole (Microtusochrogaster). *Journal of Comparative Neurology, 468*, 555–570.

Lim, M. M., & Young, L. J. (2004). Vasopressin-dependent neural circuits underlying pair bond formation in the monogamous prairie vole. *Neuroscience, 125*, 35–45.

Lindholm, C. (1995). Love as an experience of transcendence. In W. Jankowiak (Ed.), *Romantic love: A universal experience?* (pp. 57–71). New York, NY: Columbia University Press.

Lindholm, C. (1998a). Love and structure. *Theory, Culture, & Society, 15*, 243–263.

Lindholm, C. (1998b). The future of love. In V. DeMunck (Ed.), *Romantic love and sexual behavior* (pp. 17–32). Westport, CT: Praeger.

Lott, A. J., & Lott, B. E. (1961). Group cohesiveness, communication level, and conformity. *Journal of Abnormal and Social Psychology, 62*, 408–412.

Lott, A. J. & Lott, B. E. (1974). The role of reward in the formation of positive interpersonal attitudes. In T. L. Huston (Ed.), *Foundations of interpersonal attraction* (pp. 171–189). New York, NY: Academic Press.

Luo, S., Chen, H., Yue, G., Zhang, G., Zhaoyang, R., & Xu, D. (2008). Predicting marital satisfaction from self, partner, and couple characteristics: Is it me, you, or us? *Journal of Personality, 76*, 1231–1266.

Luo, S., & Zhang, G. (2009). What leads to romantic attraction: Similarity, reciprocity, security, or beauty? Evidence from a speed-dating study. *Journal of Personality, 77*, 933–964.

Madey, S. F., & Rodgers, L. (2009). The effect of attachment and Sternberg's triangular theory of love on relationship satisfaction. *Individual Differences Research, 7*(2), 76–84.

Manning, W. D., & Smock, P. J. (2002). First comes cohabitation and then comes marriage? A research note. *Journal of Family Issues, 23*, 1065–1087.

Marazziti, D., Akiskal, H. S., Rossi, A., & Cassano, G. B. (1999). Alteration of the platelet serotonin transporter in romantic love. *Psychological Medicine, 29*, 741–745.

Markey, P. M., & Markey, C. N. (2007). Romantic ideals, romantic obtainment, and relationship experiences: The complementarity of interpersonal traits among romantic partners. *Journal of Social and Personal Relationships, 24*(4), 517–533.

Maslow, A. J. (1954). *Motivation and personality.* New York, NY: Harper & Row.

Mazur, E., & Richards, L. (2011). Emerging adults' social networking online: Homophily or diversity? *Journal of Applied Developmental Psychology, 32*, 180–188.

McKnight, J., & Malcolm, J. (2000). Is male homosexuality maternally linked? *Psychology, Evolution and Gender, 2*, 229–239.

Miller, R. S. (2012). *Intimate relationships.* New York, NY: McGraw-Hill.

Mita, T. H., Dermer, M., & Knight, J. (1977). Reversed facial images and the mere-exposure hypothesis. *Journal of Personality and Social Psychology, 35*(8), 597–601.

Moreland, R. L., & Beach, S. R. (1992). Exposure effects in the classroom: The development of affinity among students. *Journal of Experimental Social Psychology, 28*, 255–276.

Morry, M. M. (2007). The attraction-similarity hypothesis among cross-sex friends: Relationship satisfaction, perceived similarities, and self-serving perceptions. *Journal of Social and Personal Relationships, 24*, 117–138.

Murdock, G. P., & White, D. (1969). Standard cross-cultural sample. *Ethology, 8*, 329–369.

Mustanski, B. S., & Bailey, J. M. (2003). A therapist's guide to the genetics of human sexual orientation. *Sexual and Relationship Therapy, 18*(4), 429–436.

Mustanski, B. S., Chivers, M. L., & Bailey, J. M. (2002). A critical review of recent biological research on human sexual orientation. *Annual Review of Sex Research, 12*, 89–140.

Myers, S. A., & Berscheid, E. (1997). The language of love: The difference a preposition makes. *Personality and Social Psychology Bulletin, 23*, 347–362.

Nakonezny, P. A., Reddick, R., & Rodgers, J. L. (2004). Did divorces decline after the Oklahoma City bombing? *Journal of Marriage and the Family, 66*, 90–100.

National Fraud Authority. (2012). *National Fraud Report 2012*. London.

Neff, L. A., & Karney, B. R. (2003). The dynamic structure of relationship perceptions: Differential importance as a strategy of relationship maintenance. *Personality and Social Psychology Bulletin, 29*, 1433–1446.

Newcomb, M. D., & Bentler, P. M. (1981). Marital breakdown. In S. Duck & R. Gilmour (Eds.), *Personal relationships 3: Personal relationships in disorder* (pp. 57–94). New York, NY: Academic Press.

Nisbett, R. E., & Wilson, T. D. (1977). The halo effect: Evidence for unconscious alteration of judgments. *Journal of Personality and Social Psychology, 35*, 250–256.

Novak, D. W., & Lerner, M. J. (1968). Rejection as a consequence of perceived similarity. *Journal of Personality and Social Psychology, 9*, 147–152.

Owen, P. R., & Laurel-Seller, E. (2000). Weight and shape ideals: Thin is dangerously in. *Journal of Applied Social Psychology, 30*(5), 979–990.

Pines, A. M. (1999). *Falling in love: Why we choose the lovers we choose*. New York, NY: Routledge.

Pines, A. M. (2001). The role of gender and culture in romantic attraction. *European Psychologist, 6*, 96–102.

Pines, A. M. (2005). *Falling in love: Why we choose the lovers we choose* (2nd ed.). New York, NY: Routledge.

PlentyofFish.com (2012, August 26). Retrieved from http://www.plentyoffish.com

Prokosch, M. D., Coss, R. G., Scheib, J. E., & Blozis, S. A. (2009). Intelligence and mate choice: Intelligent men are always appealing. *Evolution and Human Behavior, 30*, 11–20.

Pyke, K. (1999). The micropolis of care in relationships between aging parents and adult children: Individualism, collectivism, and power. *Journal of Marriage and the Family, 61*, 661–672.

Pyke, K., & Bengtson, V. L. (1996). Caring more or less: Individualistic and collectivist systems of family eldercare. *Journal of Marriage and the Family, 58*, 379–392.

Regan, P. C. (1998). Of lust and love: Beliefs about the role of sexual desire in romantic relationships. *Personal Relationships, 5*, 139–157.

Reik, T. (1944). *A psychologist looks at love*. New York, NY: Farrar & Rhinehart.

Reis, H. T., Clark, M. S., & Holmes, J. G. (2004). Perceived partner responsiveness as an organizing construct in the study of intimacy and closeness. In D. J. Mashek & P. Aron (Eds.), *Handbook of closeness and intimacy* (pp. 201–225). Mahwah, NJ: Erlbaum.

Reis, H. T., Maniaci, M. R., Caprariello, P. A., Eastwick, P. W., & Finkel, E. J. (2011). Familiarity does indeed promote attraction in live interaction. *Journal of Personality and Social Psychology, 101*, 557–570.

Reis, H. T., Nezlek, J., & Wheeler, L. (1980). Physical attractiveness in social interaction. *Journal of Personality and Social Psychology, 38*, 604–617.

Reis, H. T., & Shaver, P. (1988). Intimacy as an interpersonal process. In S. Duck (Ed.), *Handbook of personal relationships* (pp. 367–389). Chichester, UK: Wiley.

Rhoades, G. K., Kamp Dush, C. M., Atkins, D. C., Stanley, S. M., & Markman, H. J. (2011). Breaking up is hard to do: The impact of unmarried relationship dissolution on mental health and life satisfaction. *Journal of Family Psychology, 25*, 366–374.

Rhodes, G. (2006). The evolutionary psychology of facial beauty. *Annual Review of Psychology, 57*, 199–226.

Rhodes, G., Harwood, K., Yoshikawa, S., Nishitani, M., & McLean, G. (2002). The attractiveness of average facial configurations:

Cross-cultural evidence and the biology of beauty. In G. Rhodes & L. A. Zebrowitz (Eds.), *Advances in visual cognition: Vol. 1. Facial attractiveness: Evolutionary, cognitive, and social perspectives* (pp. 35–58). Westport, CT: Ablex.

Riela, S., Rodriguez, G., Aron, A., Xu, X., & Acevedo, B. P. (2010). Experiences of falling in love: Investigating culture, ethnicity, gender, and speed. *Journal of Social and Personal Relationships, 27*(4), 473–493.

Rosenberg, J., & Tunney, R. J. (2008). Human vocabulary use as display. *Evolutionary Psychology, 6*, 538–549.

Rowatt, W. C., Cunningham, M. R., & Druen, P. B. (1999). Lying to get a date: The effect of facial physical attractiveness on willing to deceive prospective dating partners. *Journal of Social and Personal Relationships, 16*, 211–225.

Ruvolo, A. P., & Ruvolo, C. M. (2000). Creating Mr. Right and Ms. Right: Interpersonal ideals and personal change in newlyweds. *Personal Relationships, 7*, 341–362.

Sampson, E. E. (1977). Psychology and the American ideal. *Journal of Personality and Social Psychology, 35*, 767–782.

Sbarra, D. A., & Emery, R. E. (2005). The emotional sequelae of nonmarital relationship dissolution: Analysis of change and intraindividual variability over time. *Personal Relationships, 12*, 213–232.

Schmitt, D. P. (2005). Is short-term mating the maladaptive result of insecure attachment? A test of competing evolutionary perspectives. *Personality and Social Psychology Bulletin, 31*, 747–768.

Schmitt, D. P. (2006). Evolutionary and cross-cultural perspectives on love: The influence of gender, personality, and local ecology on emotional investment in romantic relationships. In R. J. Sternberg & K. Weis (Eds.), *The new psychology of love* (pp. 249–273). New Haven, CT: Yale University Press.

Schmitt, D. P., Alcalay, L., Allik, J., Angleitner, A., Ault, L., Austers, I., et al. (2004). Patterns and universals of mate poaching across 53 nations: The effects of sex, culture, and personality on romantically attracting another person's partner. *Journal of Personality and Social Psychology, 86*, 560–584.

Schmitt, D. P., Alcalay, L., Allik, J., Ault, L., Austers, I., Bennett, K. L., et al. (2003). Universal sex differences in the desire for sexual variety: Tests from 52 nations, 6 continents, and 13 islands. *Journal of Personality and Social Psychology, 85*, 85–104.

Schmitt, D. P., & Buss, D. M. (2000). Sexual dimensions of person description: Beyond or subsumed by the Big Five? *Journal of Research in Personality, 34*, 141–177.

Schmitt, D. P., Youn, G., Bond, B., Brooks, S., Frye, H., Johnson, S., ... Stoka, C. (2009). When will I feel love? The effects of culture, personality, and gender on the psychological tendency to love. *Journal of Research in Personality, 43*, 830–846.

Schneider, B. H. (2000). *Friends and enemies: Peer relations in childhood.* London: Arnold.

Selfhout, M., Denissen, J., Brantje, S., & Meeus, W. (2009). In the eye of the beholder: Perceived, actual, and peer-rated similarity in personality, communication, and friendship intensity during the acquaintanceship process. *Journal of Personality and Social Psychology, 96*, 1152–1165.

Shanteau, J., & Nagy, G. (1979). Probability of acceptance in dating choice. *Journal of Personality and Social Psychology, 37*, 522–533.

Shaver, P. R., & Brennan, K. A. (1992). Attachment styles and the "Big Five" personality traits: Their connections with each other and with romantic relationship outcomes. *Personality and Social Psychology Bulletin, 18*, 536–545.

Shaver, P. R., Hazan, C., & Bradshaw, D. (1988). Love as attachment: The integration of three behavioral systems. In R. J. Sternberg & M. Barnes (Eds.), *The psychology of love* (pp. 68–99). New Haven, CT: Yale University Press.

Shaver, P. R., & Mikulincer, M. (2006). A behavioral systems approach to romantic love relationships: Attachment, caregiving, and sex. In R. J. Sternberg & K. Weis (Eds.), *The new psychology of love* (pp. 35–63). New Haven, CT: Yale University Press.

Shaver, P. R., & Mikulincer, M. (2006). Attachment theory, individual psychodynamics, and relationship functioning. In A. L. Vangelisti & D. Perlman (Eds.), *The Cambridge handbook of personal relationships* (pp. 251–271). Cambridge, UK: Cambridge University Press.

Sherwin, B. B. (1994). Sex hormones and psychological functioning in postmenopausal women. *Experimental Gerontology, 29*(3–4), 423–430.

Simon, R. W., & Barrett, A. E. (2010). Nonmarital romantic relationships and mental health in early adulthood: Does the association differ for women and men? *Journal of Health and Social Behavior, 51*, 168–182.

Simpson, J. A., Ickes, W., & Grich, J. (1999). When accuracy hurts: Reactions of anxious-ambivalent dating partners to a relationship-threatening situation. *Journal of Personality and Social Psychology, 76,* 754–769.

Singer, I. (1984). *The nature of love, Vol. 1: Plato to Luther* (2nd ed.). Chicago, IL: University of Chicago Press.

Singh, D., Dixson, B. J., Jessop, T. S., Morgan, B., & Dixson, A. F. (2010). Cross-cultural consensus for waist-hip ratio and women's attractiveness. *Evolution and Human Behavior, 31,* 176–181.

Singh, D., Yeo, S. E., Lin, P. K., & Tan, L. (2007). Multiple mediators of the attitude similarity-attraction relationship: Dominance of inferred attraction and subtlety of affect. *Basic and Applied Social Psychology, 29,* 61–74.

Snyder, M., Tanke, E. D., & Bersheid, E. (1977). Social perception and interpersonal behavior: On the self-fulfilling nature of social stereotypes. *Journal of Personality and Social Psychology, 35,* 656–666.

Sprecher, S., Aron, A., Hatfield, E., Cortese, A., Potapova, E., & Levitskaya, A. (1994). Love: American style, Russian style, and Japanese style. *Personal Relationships, 1,* 349–369.

Sprecher, S., & Fehr, B. (2011). Dispositional attachment and relationship-specific attachment as predictors of compassionate love for a partner. *Journal of Social and Personal Relationships, 28*(4), 558–574.

Stanley, S., Rhoades, G., & Markman, H. (2006). Sliding versus deciding: Inertia and the premarital cohabitation effect. *Family Relations, 55,* 499–509.

Stanley, S. M., Whitton, S. W., & Markman, H. J. (2004). Maybe I do: Interpersonal commitment and premarital or nonmarital cohabitation. *Journal of Family Issues, 25,* 496–519.

Sternberg, R. J. (1986). A triangular theory of love. *Psychological Review, 93,* 119–135.

Sternberg, R. J. (1987). Liking versus loving: A comparative evaluation of theories. *Psychological Bulletin, 102*(3), 331–345.

Sternberg, R. J. (1997). *Thinking styles.* New York, NY: Cambridge University Press.

Sternberg, R. J. (1998). *Love as a story.* Oxford, UK: Oxford University Press.

Sternberg, R. J. (2006). A duplex theory of love. In R. J. Sternberg & K. Weis (Eds.), *The new psychology of love* (pp. 184–199). New Haven, CT: Yale University Press.

Sternberg, R. J., & Barnes, M. (1985). Real and ideal others in romantic relationships: Is four a crowd? *Journal of Personality and Social Psychology, 49*, 1586–1608.

Sternberg, R. J., & Grajek, S. (1984). The nature of love. *Journal of Personality and Social Psychology, 55*, 345–356.

Sternberg, R. J., Hojjat, M., & Barnes, M. L. (2001). Empirical aspects of a theory of love as a story. *European Journal of Personality, 15*, 1–20.

Stoleru, S., Fonteille, V., Cornelis, C., Joyal, C., & Moulier, V. (2012). Functional neuroimaging studies of sexual arousal and orgasm in healthy men and women: A review and meta-analysis. *Neuroscience and Biobehavioral Reviews, 36*(4), 558–574.

Stone, E. A., Shackelford, T. K., & Buss, D. M. (2008). Socioeconomic development and shifts in mate preferences. *Evolutionary Psychology, 6*(3), 447–455.

Stone, L. (1989). Passionate attachments in the West in historical perspective. In W. Gaylin & E. Person (Eds.), *Passionate attachments: Thinking about love* (pp. 15–26). New York, NY: Touchstone.

Sugiyama, L. (2005). Physical attractiveness in adaptationist perspective. In D. M. Buss (Ed.), *The handbook of evolutionary psychology*. Hoboken, NJ: Wiley.

Swami, V., Frederick, D. A., Aavik, T., Alcalay, L., Allik, J., Anderson, D., . . . (2010). The attractive female body weight and female body dissatisfaction in 26 countries across 10 world regions: Results of the International Body Project I. *Personality and Social Psychology Bulletin, 36*, 309–325.

Tennov, D. (1979). *Love and limerence*. New York, NY: Stein & Day.

Tong, S. T., & Walther, J. B. (2010). Just say "no thanks": Romantic rejection in computer-mediated communication. *Journal of Social and Personal Relationships, 28*(4), 488–506.

Trivers, R. L. (1972). Parental investment and sexual selection. In B. Campbell (Ed.), *Sexual selection and the descent of man: 1871-1971* (pp. 136–179). Chicago, IL: Aldine.

Van Goozen, S., Wiegant, V. M., Endert, E., Helmond, F. A., & Van de Poll, N. E. (1997). Psychoendocrinological assessment of the menstrual cycle: The relationship between hormones, sexuality, and mood. *Archives of Sexual Behavior, 26*(4), 359-382.

Vaughn, D. (1990). *Uncoupling*. New York, NY: Vintage.

Waldron, V. L., & Kelley, D. I. (2008). *Communicating forgiveness*. Thousand Oaks, CA: Sage.

Wall Street Journal Online. (2012, October 1). *Why are we so rude online?* Retrieved from http://online.wsj.com/article/SB10000872396390444592404578030351784405148.html

Walster, E. H., & Walster, G. W. (1981). *A new look at love* (2nd ed.). Reading, MA: Addison-Wesley.

Walster, E. H., Walster, G. W., & Berscheid, E. (1978). *Equity: Theory and research*. Boston, MA: Allyn & Bacon.

Wedekind, C., Seebeck, T., Bettens, F., & Paepke, A. J. (1995). MHC-dependent mate preferences in humans. *Proceedings: Biological Sciences, 260*(1359), 245–249.

Weisskirch, R. S., & Delevi, R. (2012). Its ovr b/n u n me: Technology use, attachment styles, and gender roles in relationship dissolution. *Cyberpsychology, Behavior, and Social Networking, 15*(9), 486–490.

Wendorf, C. A., Lucas, T., Imamoglu, E. O., Weisfeld, C. C., & Weisfeld, G. E. (2011). Marital satisfaction across three cultures: Does the number of children have an impact after accounting for other marital demographics? *Journal of Cross-Cultural Psychology, 42*(3), 340–354.

White, J. K., Hendrick, S. S., & Hendrick, C. (2004). Big Five personality variables and relationship constructs. *Personality and Individual Differences, 37*, 1519–1530.

White, S. G., & Hatcher, C. (1984). Couple complementarity and similarity: A review of the literature. *American Journal of Family Therapy, 12*, 15–25.

Whitty, M. T., & Buchanan, T. (2012). The online romance scam: A serious cybercrime. *Cyberpsychology, Behavior, and Social Networking, 15*(3), 181–183.

Whitty, M. T., & Carr, A. (2006). *Cyberspace romance: The psychology of online relationships*. New York, NY: Palgrave Macmillan.

Willis, J. & Todorov, A. (2006). First impressions: Making up your mind after a 100 ms exposure to a face. *Psychological Science, 17*, 592–598.

Woods, L. N., & Emery, R. E. (2002). The cohabitation effects on divorce: Causation or selection? *Journal of Divorce and Remarriage, 37*, 101–119.

Zajonc, R. B. (1968). Attitudinal effects of mere exposures. *Journal of Personality and Social Psychology, 9*, 1–27.

Zajonc, R. B. (2001). Mere exposure: A gateway to the subliminal. *Current Directions in Psychological Science, 10*, 224–228.

Zajonc, R. B., Adelmann, P. K., Murphy, S. T., & Niedenthal, P. M. (1987). Convergence in the physical appearance of spouses: An implication of the vascular theory of emotional efference. *Motivation and Emotion, 11*(4), 335–346.

Zhou, W., & Chen, D. (2009). Sociochemosensory and emotional functions: Behavioral evidence for shared mechanisms. *Psychological Science, 20*, 1118–1124.

Zimmerman, C. (2009). Dissolution of relationships, breakup strategies. In H. T. Reis & S. Sprecher (Eds.), *Encyclopedia of human relationships* (pp. 434–435). Thousand Oaks, CA: Sage.

Index

agape, 39–40
agreeableness, 158
appreciation, 122–123
attachment theory
  in adults, 25–27
  attachment styles, 25
  background, 24–25
  behavioral systems, 27–30
  and emotional attachment, 73
  in relationship maintenance, 122
attraction
  as antecedent to love, 5
  benefits of, 107–108
  dissimilarity, 98–99
  familiarity, 93–94
  gender differences, 103, 105
  influence of, 91
  personality
    assumptions, based on attractiveness, 107
    traits, desirable, 101–102
  physical appearance
    body characteristics, 105
    facial characteristics, 103–104
    primacy of, 18–19, 102
  proximity, 92–93
  reciprocity, 99–100
  role of, 30
  similarity
    in demographics, 96
    inferences about, 97–98
    in personality, 95–96
    to self-perception, 96–97
    values, 97
    universality, 106

background, love
  evolutionary role of, 31
  importance of, 2–3, 11–13
  versus liking, 10–11
  study of
    clinical approaches, 9–10
    cognitive-consistency theories, 7–9
    literary approaches, 4–5
    philosophic approaches, 3–4
    reinforcement theories, 5–7
balance theory, 8
behavioral systems
  attachment, 28
  attraction, role of, 30
  brain systems, 30
  caregiving, 29
  and hormones, 30
  sexual, 29
  strategies for, 27–28

INDEX

Berscheid, Ellen, 6–7, 55. *See also* Berscheid's four kinds of love
Berscheid's four kinds of love
  attachment, 56
  background, 55
  companionate, 56–57, 113–114
  compassionate, 56, 115
  romantic, 57
Big Five theory
  agreeableness, 158
  conscientiousness, 158–160
  definition, 157
  desirable, 101–102
  extraversion, 160
  neuroticism, 160–161
  openness to experience, 161
biological perspectives on love
  adaptive traits, 16
  attachment theory
    in adults, 25–27
    attachment styles, 25
    background, 24–25
    behavioral systems, 27–30
  brain mechanisms
    hormones and, 31, 33
    mate preference, 31
    obsessive-compulsive disorder, 33–34
  decision-making biases
    dynamic nature of, 23
    gender challenges, 22
    intimacy, 22–23
    levels of significance, 24
  evolution, 15–16
  evolutionary psychology, 16–17
  experience of, men versus women
  purpose, 17
  universality, 18
  sexual preferences, 19
  genetics, in sexual preference, 20
  love, role of, 19
  sexual orientation, 20–21
Bowlby, John, 24–25, 27
brain mechanisms
  dopamine, 31, 33
  mate preference, 31
  norepinephrine, 33
  obsessive-compulsive disorder, 33–34
  in romantic love, 31–32
  serotonin, 31, 33
  ventral tegmental area, 33
Brand, Rebecca, 146
breakups, nonmarital
  communication of, 126
  ill effects of, 125–126
  reasons for, 125
Buss, David, 71
Byrne, Donn, 6

challenges in relationships. *See* relationships, challenges
cheating, 163–164
children and marital satisfaction
  conflict, exacerbation of, 74
  stabilization, 74–75
Clark, Margaret, 50. *See also* communal responsiveness as love
clinical approaches, 9–10
Clore, Jerry, 6

cognitive-consistency theories, 7–9
cohabitation
　duration of, 119
　increase in, 118–119
　and marriage, 119–120
　statistics, 120
collectivism and culture
　definition, 68–69
　family bonds, 69
　gender role in, 69
　self-perception, 70
commitment, 44–45, 123, 165–166
communal responsiveness as love
　definition, 50
　examples, 50–51
　expectations versus reality, 53
　forms of, 51–52
　hierarchies of, 52–53
　noncontingency, 52
　successful, 51
　threshold of strength, 53
communication, 169–170
companionate love, 56–57, 113–114
compassionate love, 56, 115
conscientiousness, 158–160
construction of love scale, 82
　limits, 79
　reasons for, 78–79
　steps
　　content validity, 83
　　external validation, 85–86
　　face validity, 83
　　internal validation, 85
　　items, construction of, 82
　　reliability, 84
　　standardization, 86–88
　　theory formation, 81–82
　　Sternberg Triangular Love Scale, 80–81
content validity of love scale construction, 83
cultural differences, romantic love, 63–66
cultural perspectives of love
　children and marital satisfaction
　　conflict, exacerbation of, 74
　　stabilization, 74–75
　collectivism
　　definition, 68–69
　　family bonds, 69
　　gender role in, 69
　　self-perception, 70
　impact on experience of love
　　cultural differences, 70–71
　　emotional attachment, 71–73
　individualism
　　definition, 67
　　and family, 68
　　in relationships, 67–68
　　self-perception, 70
　romantic love
　　characteristics of, 65–66
　　core of, 64–65
　　cultural differences, 63–66
　　experience of, 64
　　falling in love, reasons for, 61–62
　　gender differences, 62–63
　　perceptions of, 66
　　universality of, 59–61

Darwin, Charles, 15
decision-making biases
  dynamic nature of, 23
  gender challenges, 22
  intimacy, 22–23
  levels of significance, 24
Diagnostic and Statistical Manual of Mental Disorders, third edition (DSM-III), 20
Dion, Karen, 67
Dion, Keith, 67
divorce
  and attachment theory, 129
  disasters, role of, 128–129
  reasons for, 127
  remarriage, 129–130
  statistics on, 126–127
dopamine, 31, 33
DSM-III. See *Diagnostic and Statistical Manual of Mental Disorders, third edition*
duplex theory of love
  commitment, 44–45
  correlation between triangle and stories, 50
  intimacy, 44–45
  passion, 44–45
  as a story
    advantages and disadvantages, 49–50
    examples, 48
    as predictor of satisfaction, 49–50
    restriction of horizons, 49
    types of stories, 47–48
  as a triangle
    combinations possible, 44–45
    feelings, nonaccord with actions, 46–47
    kinds of love, 45
    types of triangles, 46

emotional attachment
  and attachment styles, 73
  and stress level, 72
equity theory, 7
eros, 38
evolution, 15–16, 31
evolutionary psychology, 16–17
evolution of sexual preferences, 19
experience of love
  cultural differences, 70–71
  emotional attachment, 71–73
external validation of love scale construction, 85–86
extraversion, 160

face validity of love scale construction, 83
Fisher, H. E., 135
forgiveness, 124
Freud, Sigmund, 9
friendship
  choosing, 54–55
  communal responsiveness, 54
  Internet as tool for, 55

gender differences
  attraction, 18–19, 103, 105
  collectivism, 69
  in decision making, 22
  in romantic love, 32, 42–43, 62–63
genetics, in sexual preference, 20

Hatfield, Elaine, 2, 114
Heider, Fritz, 8
Hendrick, Clyde, 37, 40. *See also* romantic love, styles
Hendrick, Susan, 37, 40. *See also* romantic love, styles
Homans, George, 6

individualism and culture
  definition, 67
  and family, 68
  in relationships, 67–68
  self-perception, 70
internal validation of love scale
  construction, 85
International Sexuality Description Project (ISDP), 71–72
intimacy, 44–45
ISDP. *See* International Sexuality Description Project
item construction, of love scale, 82

jealousy, 168–169

Kendall, Todd, 128
Kenrick, Douglas, 22, 24

Lee, John Allen, 37–38. *See also* romantic love, styles
Lott, Al, 5–6
Lott, Bernice, 5–6
Love Attitudes Scale, 40–42
ludus, 38

maintenance of relationships
  appreciation, 122–123
  and attachment, 122
  commitment, 123
  forgiveness, 124
  necessity of, 121–122
  positive illusions, 123–124
  Relational Maintenance Model, 122
mania, 38–39
marital satisfaction, children and
  conflict, exacerbation of, 74
  stabilization, 74–75
Maslow, Abraham, 9–10
mate preference, 31

neuroticism, 160–161
norepinephrine, 33

online dating
  advantages of, 132–133
  versus conventional dating, 136–137
  dangers
    personal safety, 149–150
    scams, 148
  description of, 132
  effectiveness
    communication, 138
    experiential factors, 137–138
    information overload, 138
    of matching process, 139–140
    of promises, 141
    selection factors, 137
  leveling the playing field
    assumptions about, 143

online dating (*cont.*)
- first name impressions, 144–145
- photos, impact of, 145–146
- text, correlated with appearance, 146–147
- matching services
  - by compatibility, 134–135
  - core traits, 135
  - other criteria, 135–136
- rejection, management of, 142–143
- rules, 133–134
- types of services, 132

openness to experience, 161. *See also* Big Five theory

Origin of Species, The (Darwin), 15

passion, 44–45, 164–165
personality
- assumptions about, based on attractiveness, 107
- similarity versus complementarity debate
  - advantages and disadvantages of each, 156–157
  - complementarity, basis for, 152–153
  - love as a story, implications of, 153–154
  - similarity, basis for, 152
  - stories, types, 154–155
  - and styles of thinking, 155–156
- traits
  - Big Five theory, 157
  - agreeableness, 158
  - conscientiousness, 158–160
  - desirable, 101–102
  - extraversion, 160
  - neuroticism, 160–161
  - openness to experience, 161

physical appearance
- body characteristics, 105
- facial characteristics, 103–104
- primacy of, 18–19, 102

Plato, 3
pragma, 39
Proxmire, Senator William, 2

reinforcement theories, 5–7
Relational Maintenance Model, 122
relationships, challenges
- cheating, 163–164
- commitment, 165–166
- communication, 169–170
- expectations, 171
- jealousy, 168–169
- passion, loss of, 164–165
- previous relationships, 167–168

relationships, development of
- companionate, 113–114
- compassionate, 115
- romantic, 114–115

relationships, maintenance of
- appreciation, 122–123
- and attachment, 122
- commitment, 123
- forgiveness, 124
- necessity of, 121–122
- positive illusions, 123–124
- Relational Maintenance Model, 122

relationships, stages
  breakups, nonmarital
    communication of, 126
    ill effects of, 125–126
    reasons for, 125
  with cohabitation
    duration of, 119
    increase in, 118–119
    and marriage, 119–120
    statistics, 120
  divorce
    and attachment theory, 129
    disasters, role of, 128–129
    reasons for, 127
    remarriage, 129–130
    statistics on, 126–127
  maintenance
    appreciation, 122–123
    and attachment, 122
    commitment, 123
    forgiveness, 124
    necessity of, 121–122
    positive illusions, 123–124
    Relational Maintenance Model, 122
  speed dating
    cues used, 117–118
    definition, 116
    physical attractiveness, role in, 117
reliability of love scale construction, 84
romantic love
  characteristics of, 65–66
  versus companionate love, 57
  core of, 64–65
  cultural differences, 63–66
  experience of, 64
  falling in love, reasons for, 61–62
  gender differences, 32, 42–43, 62–63
  perceptions of, 66
  and personality, 42
  primary styles of, 38
  readiness for, 32
  relationship maintenance of, 114–115
  research on, 37–38
  satisfaction with, 43
  secondary styles, 38–39
  sexual attitudes and, 42
  styles of
    assessment of, 41
    conflicts of, 39–40
    gender differences, 42–43
    Love Attitudes Scale, 40–42
    and personality, 42
    primary, 38
    research on, 37–38
    satisfaction with, 43
    secondary, 38–39
    sexual attitudes, 42
  universality of, 59–61

Schmidt, David, 71–72
serotonin, 31, 33
sexual orientation, 20–21
sexual preferences, evolution of, 19
Shaver, P. R., 25, 26–27, 28
similarity versus complementarity debate
  advantages and disadvantages of each, 156–157

similarity versus (*cont.*)
  complementarity, basis for, 152–153
  love as a story, implications of, 153–154
  similarity, basis for, 152
  stories, types, 154–155
  and styles of thinking, 155–156
speed dating
  cues used, 117–118
  definition, 116
  physical attractiveness, role in, 117
stages of relationships. *See* relationships, stages
standardization of love scale construction, 86–88
Sternberg, Robert, 44. *See also* duplex theory of love
Sternberg Triangular Love Scale, 80–81
stories, role in relationships
  advantages and disadvantages, 49–50
  examples, 48
  implications for love, 153–154
  as predictor of satisfaction, 49–50
  restriction of horizons, 49
  types of stories, 47–48, 154–155
storge, 38
styles of romantic love. *See* romantic love, styles of
Symposium (Plato), 3

taxonomic approaches to love
  background, 35–36
  Berscheid's four kinds of love
    attachment, 56
    background, 55
    companionate, 56–57
    compassionate, 56
    romantic, 57
  communal responsiveness as definition, 50
    examples, 50–51
    expectations versus reality, 53
    forms of, 51–52
    hierarchies of, 52–53
    noncontingency, 52
    successful, 51
    threshold of strength, 53
  definition, 36–37
  duplex theory of love
    correlation between triangle and stories, 50
    as a story
      advantages and disadvantages, 49–50
      examples, 48
      as predictor of satisfaction, 49–50
      restriction of horizons, 49
      types of stories, 47–48
    as a triangle
      combinations possible, 44–45
      feelings, nonaccord with actions, 46–47
      kinds of love, 45
      types of triangles, 46

friendship
   choosing, 54–55
   communal responsiveness, 54
   Internet as tool for, 55
  romantic love, styles
   assessment of, 41
   conflicts of, 39–40
   gender differences, 42–43
   Love Attitudes Scale, 40–42
   and personality, 42
   primary, 38
   research on, 37–38
   satisfaction with, 43
   secondary, 38–39
   sexual attitudes, 42
Tennov, Dorothy, 10
theory formation of love scale construction, 81–82

Tong, Stephanie, 142
traits, personality
   Big Five theory, 157
   agreeableness, 158
   conscientiousness, 158–160
   desirable, 101–102
   extraversion, 160
   neuroticism, 160–161
   openness to experience, 161

universality of romantic love, 59–61

ventral tegmental area, 33

Waither, Joseph, 142
Walster, Elaine, 6–7
Walster, G. W., 6–7

www.ingramcontent.com/pod-product-compliance
Ingram Content Group UK Ltd.
Pitfield, Milton Keynes, MK11 3LW, UK
UKHW021829140426
5217IPUK00021B/1349